ROCK and POP elevens

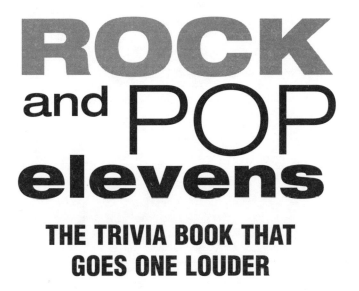

ROCK and POP elevens

THE TRIVIA BOOK THAT GOES ONE LOUDER

Simon Trewin, Tom Bromley
& Michael Moran

Michael O'Mara Books Ltd

First published in Great Britain in 2004 by
Michael O'Mara Books Ltd
9 Lion Yard, Tremadoc Road
London SW4 7NQ

A CIP catalogue record for this book is available from the British Library.

ISBN 1-84317-112-0

1 3 5 7 9 10 8 6 4 2

www.mombooks.com

Designed and typeset by E-Type

Printed and bound in England by Clays Ltd, St Ives plc

For Nigel Tufnel

CONTENTS

* (ish)

Hello, Cleveland

Blinded by Science

Let's Talk about Sex

I'm with the Band

Media Whores

Filthy Lucre

Into the Groove

Spliffs and Stiffs

Discellany

Introduction

(with apologies to *This is Spiñal Tap*)

Hello. Our names are Simon Trewin, Tom Bromley and Michael Moran. We're writers. We do a lot of books. The story about the little boy with the lightning scar who goes to wizard school? That was ours. We wish.

So in the late fall of 2003, when we felt the world was ready for a rock 'n' roll trivia book with a difference, we jumped at the chance to write the miscellany – the, if you will, discellany – that you're about to read. We wanted to capture the sights, the sounds, the smells, of the hard-working world of rock 'n' roll. And we got that. But we got more, a lot more.

This is a very special rock 'n' roll trivia book. Because as you will see, the numbers all go to eleven. Right across the board. Eleven sections, eleven lists, eleven points, eleven . . . eleven . . . eleven. Other trivia books – and there are plenty of them – they all go up to ten. Top Ten this, Top Ten that, Top Ten whatever. Where can you go from there? Exactly. Nowhere. This is the book that gives you that extra little push over the cliff. The rock 'n' roll essential reference book that is, simply, one louder. But hey – enough of our yakkin'.

Whaddaya say, let's boogie!

Simon, Tom and Michael, October 2004

THE BANDS

Eleven Band Names and their Origins

For a new band, the selection of the name is a pivotal decision. A poster or flyer must tell audiences exactly what to expect, so anything too vague is out. Equally, too specific a name might prove restrictive for future growth, once skiffle gives way to psychedelia (or vice versa) . . .

Blue Öyster Cult
First of all, there's a colour. It has no meaning, nor function; it just sits there being a colour. They add Oyster to the mix, perhaps subtly hinting at the crucial importance of their leader, Sandy Pearlman, or perhaps referring to a New York seafood restaurant that the band were known to frequent. Finally, they round the name off with Cult, complete with its baggage of secrecy and possible Satanism. The improvement over their preceding *nom de rock*, Soft White Underbelly, is near incalculable.

Ultimately, though, Blue Öyster Cult's enduring contribution to rock history is the innovation of the superfluous umlaut. Poised teutonically atop their name, majestic and pointless, it marked out a path which luminaries like Motörhead, Mötley Crüe, Queensrÿche and, of course, the legendary Spiñal Tap followed to glory. BOC, we salute you.

Fabian
First of the one-name solo stars, like Lulu, Madonna and Orville after him. Born Fabian Fabiano Forte Bonaparte, he shortened his name presumably in order to avoid offending any survivors of the Napoleonic Wars. The decision seems to have paid off – according to our detailed research, no such complaints have to date been received.

The Teardrop Explodes
Most people know that this name comes from a 1970s Marvel comic. Specifically it's from *Daredevil*, issue 77, June 1971. Singer Julian Cope read the following extraordinary account of the submariner Prince Namor detonating an anomalous apparition and knew at once that he'd found a name to be reckoned with: 'Filling the wintered glades of Central Park

with an unearthly whine . . . painting the leaf-bare branches with golden fire . . . THE TEARDROP EXPLODES!' Well, it's certainly got a bit more to it than Wham!.

REM
In contrast to their elliptical and frequently inaudible lyrics, this Georgia beat combo's name requires very little explanation: REM, or Rapid Eye Movement, was selected over some of the other candidates – such as Slut Bank and the housewives' favourite Cans of Piss. To this day the group have a somewhat casual relationship with their name and frequently abandon it for a bewildering array of aliases, including William, Hornets Attack Victor Mature, and Bingo Handjob. All terrible names, it's true – but all major improvements on Cans of Piss. That one still worries us.

Extreme Noise Terror
This easygoing country band, whose members comprise an extended Mormon family, are frequent performers at Nashville's famed Grand Old Opry and favourites of former US President Gerald Ford. Well, no, of course that isn't the case – but wouldn't it be lovely if it was?

The Beach Boys
Brian Wilson and Co. recorded their first single, 'Surfin'', as The Pendletones. A pendletone was a sort of heavy plaid top, designed for outdoor workers like lumberjacks but adopted by surfers. When damp, a pendletone smells a bit like a wet dog. Perhaps it was for this reason that A&R man Joe Saraceno, who was charged with organizing the distribution of this 45, liked the record but hated the name. Joe picked The Beach Boys on a whim. A few weeks later a box of singles arrived at the Wilsons' home; the brothers excitedly tore open the package to find that they weren't called The Pendletones any more.

Prefab Sprout
Wilfully bad. Supposedly based on a misheard Nancy Sinatra lyric, this dreadful appellation represents a complete misapprehension of the very nature of rock 'n' roll.

Pearl Jam
Supposedly named after singer Eddie Vedder's grandma Pearl and her hallucinogenic preserves. And there we were thinking it was something to do with semen. Was that just us?

William Burroughs
It is not William Burroughs' music that concerns us here so much as it is the extraordinary number of groups that have ill-advisedly taken

inspiration for their names from his writings. A far from exhaustive search yields: Soft Machine, The Soft Boys, Steely Dan, Dead Fingers Talk, Heavy Metal Kids, The Mugwumps, Naked Lunch, Nova Mob, Sex Gang Children and Thin White Rope. You will observe that, with one notable exception, these chosen names have not led to fame and riches for the bearers.

Babylon Zoo

Babylon Zoo might seem an odd choice, until sole member Jas Mann explains: 'Babylon is before the enslavement in a paradise thought, but in this present society we are Frankenstein and the monster is biting back at us, so it's become a zoo.' Ah, that's cleared that up. Thanks, Jas.

Oasis

Possibly named after: a Manchester clothes shop, a Burnage minicab service, Bonehead's local Indian takeaway, or – most plausibly – a leisure centre in North Star Avenue, Swindon. The Oasis Centre, despite its small size, has staged concerts by such luminaries as Status Quo (with support act T'Pau) and, significantly, The Inspiral Carpets. Noel Gallagher was certainly in the Inspirals' road crew when they played there.

Eleven Infant Prodigies

Ever since the days of prodigies like Mozart, Paganini, and Frankie Lymon, musical audiences have been simultaneously fascinated and repelled by these pocket-sized geniuses who seem to have been born with abilities the rest of us can acquire only after years of practice. And *then* we're told we're too old . . .

Stevie Wonder

When his first hit album, *The 12 Year Old Genius,* topped the US charts in 1963, 'Little' Stevie Wonder was thirteen. It's never too soon to start lying about your age.

Musical Youth

Midlands scallywags whose precocious talent was made slightly more bearable by their rapid descent into ignominy. Guitarist Kelvin Grant was nine years old when their solitary hit, 'Pass the Dutchie', reached the top of the UK charts – and he was already a better musician than any of us are now.

St Winifred's School Choir
There may not have been anyone quite like Grandma. There's no one quite like this lot any more, thank God.

Grange Hill
'Just Say No.' That's what they said. (Except for Zammo. He said, 'Just say, "Not just yet, thanks – let me finish making this annoying record first."') Nancy Reagan approved and invited the gang to the White House, where they made full use of the spacious, well-appointed restrooms.

Helen Shapiro
Even at fourteen, when she began her career, she managed to look like your mum. Forty years later she still does.

Hanson
Each one with his own unique image – the Hippie Kid, the Hot Chick, the Cowardly Lion – the three Hanson boys ruled the airwaves for a brief period in the mid-nineties. Drummer Zack Hanson was nine at the time. Didn't he have any, like, *homework* to do?

Silverchair
Sort of a bit like Nirvana, but with Clearasil instead of heroin.

Debbie Gibson
Wrote and recorded a US number one ('Foolish Beat') at sixteen, which is something of an achievement. Debbie says: 'I'm very driven, even though I can't drive.'

Kate Bush
Uncharacteristically, for a multinational corporation, EMI nurtured the young Kate Bush with considerable patience, releasing her first single after two whole years of development, when she was a grand old lady of seventeen.

Little Jimmy Osmond
Started out as the most annoying seven-year-old ever to be awarded a gold record. Ended up fairly sane, apparently.

Michael Jackson
Started out as the most promising ten-year-old ever to release a record. Ended up a llama-owner of some repute.

Eleven Rock Stars and How they Measure Up (Part One)

When rock stars disport themselves on our television screens, or on concert stages, looking so ineffably *cool*, it's nice to think that we must be in some way better than them: either taller, or less gangly, or *something*. Here, therefore, is an exhausting – if not exhaustive – table of rock star heights (or lack thereof).

Pat Benatar: 5 ft
Love is a battlefield. With very shallow trenches, we hope.

Stevie Nicks: 5 ft 1 in
Excessive frills and, indeed, furbelows in no way detract from the minuteness of the object.

Prince: 5 ft 2 in
Purple popster's predilection for pocket-sized paramours projects paranoia, perchance?

Davy Jones: 5 ft 3 in
Although he always looked silly with that great big tambourine (will he play it or jump through it?), we can't help liking Dave.

Paul Simon: 5ft 3 in
If he hadn't hooked up with lofty soprano and restaurateur Garfunkel we might never have noticed.

Elton John: 5 ft 3½ in
Mister John is five foot three *and a half*, if you don't mind!

Cher: 5 ft 4 in
One of those ones who you think will be tall, and then suddenly isn't.

Boy George: 6 ft
You haven't known fear until George comes up to you wearing a dress and you realize how irrefutably *huge* he is.

Roger Waters: 6 ft 4 in
Brainy, tall, and always a little bit cross. One to avoid.

David Hasselhoff: 6 ft 4 in
Actor whose singing career leads to him being 'big in Germany' (and a rapper) beats Roger by dint of his lovely curly hair.

Mick Fleetwood: 6 ft 5 in
We'd blame it on the hat, if he didn't insist on standing next to Stevie Nicks, Sam Fox, us . . .

Eleven Ever-Changing Rock Line-Ups

When considering bands with the most prodigious turnover of line-up, we have deliberately excluded those recording acts (So Solid Crew, Wu-Tang Clan, Royal Scots Dragoon Guards) with a membership so vast that no one, not even the band members, is quite sure who else is in the group.

Rainbow
Essentially a vehicle for the talents of electric-guitar firebrand Ritchie Blackmore, Rainbow, with at least twenty-three musicians over the last thirty years, have perhaps the best-oiled revolving door in rock. Maybe it's just that little Welshman's hat he insists on wearing.

Black Sabbath
Beating Rainbow in terms of sheer numbers, but edged into second place for taking slightly too long about it, the act we now call 'Ozzy's old band' have employed a staggering twenty-eight members since they collapsed on to the scene in 1968.

Wishbone Ash
Host to some nineteen souls over the years. Still touring, still playing 'Blowin' Free' and still changing bass players more often than you change your pants.

Jethro Tull
When quizzed about their profligate consumption of musicians, Ian Anderson is quoted as saying, 'Lots of different reasons. Some of the boys left to get married, settle down, form their own bands, that sort of thing.' He fails to mention any members who left to become a lady.

Yes
More volatile than their even-dozen names might suggest. Apart from the shock tactic of a temporary merger with The Buggles in the early 1980s,

they have also seen the hugely talented but prodigiously thirsty Rick Wakeman leave and return at least twice, and the formation of Anderson Bruford Wakeman Howe – who might as well have been Yes, were it not for some tiresome legal proceedings.

Fairport Convention
Fairport's total membership hovers around the twenty-four mark, but they get points docked for having far too many fiddlers, hurdy-gurdy men and landscape gardeners to be considered a proper rock act.

The Red Hot Chili Peppers
Perhaps it was that thing with the socks. For whatever reason, thirteen men have been part of this four-piece band since their inception in 1983.

Journey
For such a successful act, very little is known about Journey. Perhaps the only people qualified to tell you about this AOR juggernaut are the ten musicians to have passed through the band. But they won't. They're all too busy practising *scales* and such.

AC/DC
A score of at least seventeen for the School Disco fashion pioneers.

The Steve Miller Band
Everyone loves 'The Joker'. Someone steals its signature riff at least once a year. And twenty-four young men have played it.

Santana
Ladies and gentlemen, we have a winner. Upwards of sixty-one members since the band's inception in 1969. That's not counting the additional eighteen personnel listed under 'special guests'. And Carlos seems like such an easygoing chap.

Eleven Vintage Hit-Makers

Louis Armstrong
Born in 1901, Louis had formed his first band by 1917. There wasn't even a proper Top Forty for another thirty-five years. While he was waiting for that, Louis kept himself busy puffing his cheeks out and reinventing the idea of popular music. In 1964 he had a hit with 'Hello,

Dolly' even though he'd forgotten recording it. Finally, in February 1968, he had a number one with 'What a Wonderful World'. He was not quite sixty-seven.

Cher
Cher was fifty-two years and seven months when she hit the number-one spot with 'Believe' in 1999. By the time the record was released she'd had a hit TV show and six tattoos, won an Oscar, and had herself extensively remodelled until she looked like a sort of gazelle-lady: all things we wish *we'd* done.

John Lee Hooker
John Lee Hooker was born in 1920, but falsified his records in order to appear old enough to join the US army. We're not sure that the extra three years makes a whole lot of difference either way, as comparatively few gentlemen in their mid-seventies have made Top Forty records. Luckily for Mr Hooker, he had Van Morrison along for the ride on 'Gloria' in 1993.

Andy Williams
Aged seventy-four, Andy felt he needed a little support on a retread of his classic 'Can't Take My Eyes Off You'. He chose as his duet partner/nurse the distressingly ebullient Denise Van Outen.

Ronnie Biggs
Train-robber Ronnie was drafted in as a temporary replacement for Johnny Rotten during The Sex Pistols' last desperate months in 1979. Ronnie, born in 1929, was a little too old to be considered part of the punk-rock generation but was accorded punk status by dint of his swearing ability and willingness to wear a handkerchief on his head.

Father Abraham
No one is entirely sure quite how old the mysterious DJ and Smurfs front-man is. The length of his beard implies a prodigious vintage, and the funny little bowler hat he wears suggests the indifference to public opinion that comes only with real maturity or membership of an extreme Ulster Protestant sect.

Gordon Haskell
Former Flowerpot Man and Cupid's Inspiration Gordon was (briefly) in King Crimson at the beginning of the seventies. Then, aged fifty-five, he narrowly missed the number-one spot in 2001 with 'How Wonderful You Are'.

Frank Sinatra

Another singer whose hits predate the notion of a singles chart, Frank had his last stand in the Top Forty at the age of seventy-eight. As a man in failing health, The Hoboken canary no doubt appreciated the stocky, pugilistic figure of Bono at his side when 'I've Got You Under My Skin' made number four in December 1993.

The Rolling Stones

When their most recent hit, 'Don't Stop', charted, both Mick and Keith were fifty-nine and Charlie Watts a slightly more impressive sixty-one. Bill Wyman, the oldest Stone, had long since departed for the less taxing life of a restaurateur.

Charles Aznavour

Aznavour's career began in 1941 and he was still recording in 2001. During this time he worked with Edith Piaf, Juliette Greco and Pia Zadora. None of these people are strictly rock 'n' roll, it's true – but Charles was born in 1924 and rock 'n' roll wasn't really invented until he was thirty, so you can't really blame him for that.

Telly Savalas

Born in 1922, Telly spent two weeks at number one in 1975 with his spoken version of the old Bread hit 'If'. He had no subsequent hits, but the TV character he helped create remains to this day a pejorative term for any man afflicted by male pattern baldness.

Eleven Haircuts of Rock

When considering the role of the haircut in rock, perhaps the most important and far-reaching innovation is the development of the mullet. The 'business out front, party in the back' concept has much more to offer than its more one-dimensional predecessors (the quiff, the pageboy, the mess) could ever hope to match. Although we also cover work by hair innovators working on dual-function coiffure outside the mullet framework, there is only one hairdo that says it all and does it all.

Ray Dorset

For many people the only member of Mungo Jerry, Ray owes his persistence in the public memory to his accessorization of the basic Afro with two of the most prodigious mutton chops deployed since the Charge of the Light Brigade.

Cyndi Lauper
One of the foremost proponents of the mess. This multicoloured, multilayered, multipurpose hairstyle served at once to insulate the fevered Lauper brain and as a camouflaged refuge for brightly coloured tropical birds.

Martin Gore
A variant on the Ray Dorset/Mick Farren Euro-Afro, Martin's slick-sided dandelion-puffball concept also doubled as a handy timepiece for the more *confused* members of Depeche Mode.

Kajagoogoo
Candidates for inclusion on the strength of singer Limahl's piebald mullet, the fleetingly fashionable eighties popsters clinched their position with bassist Nick Beggs' hairdo/abacus combo. Equally useful for shaking at impressionable young girls and calculating Kaja's vanishingly tiny royalties.

Roy Wood
Ostensibly a straightforward rainbow wreck (see Cyndi Lauper), Roy's mess was twinned with a matching beard, making it an unattainable dream for women, or children, or men with colour vision and a modicum of taste.

Mike Score
Mike's haircut was the focal point of A Flock of Seagulls, and many have tried and failed to explain the possible thinking behind it. Whether it truly was an evocation of avian mystery in the medium of hair, no one will ever know. Well, not unless they ask Mike.

Phil Oakey
Proud owner of a hairdo comprising equal parts Veronica Lake and Alan Ladd, Phil played peekaboo with his audiences for far longer than seemed necessary, or even funny.

Robert Smith
Robert is indisputably the high priest of the übermess, which first began to take shape after a particularly rough night out on the shandy with Siouxsie and the Banshees. It expanded until it colonized other Cure members' heads in search of adequate *Lebensraum*.

Dee Snider
When all about him were backcombing their locks into major fire hazards,

Twisted Sister front-man Snider cultivated little blond ringlets hitherto seen only on annoying girls in *Just William* books. His pioneering hair-and-make-up legacy is now safe in the hands of Christina Aguilera.

Joe Strummer – the Travis Bickle years
The owner of the most conservative hairstyle in punk, Joe appeared on the covers of the last couple of Clash singles with an inch-wide strip of hair down the centre of his scalp – a sort of rock 'n' roll Brazilian. A few months later Joe reappeared with his original radical-accountant style restored to its rightful place atop one of the wisest heads in music.

At last – the mullet
Many lay claim to having invented the mullet. In fact recent research undertaken for this book proves that former Beatles bassist Paul McCartney devised the look some years ago. Paul, always by far the most innovative and experimental Beatle, had cultivated a neck-warming back-fringe by the winter of 1971. Referring to the resulting adornment as his 'Wings of Pegasus', he evidently took great pride in the development – going so far as to name his band after it.

Eleven Bands that were One Louder

To a sane listener, going to see the 'world's loudest band' seems at best a somewhat dubious pleasure. Nevertheless, many bands advertise themselves as such, so clearly there is some perceived merit for sheer volume. Here, then, is a list of bands who apparently agree.

The Pretty Things
The band who out-rolled The Stones throughout the early part of the 1960s; the dirtiest, hairiest, nastiest, loudest band the world had seen to date.

Deep Purple
The first act to be officially accredited with the 'loudest band in the world' title. Within a year of winning that highest of honours, they split. The responsibility of maintaining such an ear-splitting standard was evidently too much to bear.

The Who
With both Pete Townshend and the late John Entwistle suffering significant hearing loss, no one could accuse The Who of allowing concern for their personal well-being stand in the way of their pursuit of long and

lasting loudness. In 1976 they took over Purple's mantle as the world's loudest band. Unlike numerous bean-eaters and fish-jugglers, the band weren't invited on to Roy Castle's *Record Breakers* to demonstrate their feat.

Grand Funk Railroad
Neither particularly funky nor having any direct influence over rail transportation in their native Flint, Michigan, Grand Funk maintained a reputation for directness, simplicity and out-and-out noisiness that endeared them to the brawnier end of America's 1970s rock audience.

Motörhead
Motörhead have led the field for many years in terms of sonic assault, speed-freak craziness and sheer umlaut use. Throughout their long and deafening career, vicar's son Ian 'Lemmy' Kilminster has remained a standard bearer for all enthusiasts of the sideburn and the wart. He also assures us that Motörhead are loud enough to wake someone out of a coma: 'Back in, what was it, 1980, I think. Or '81. This kid was in a hospital after his back was crushed, in a coma. And we made a tape, you know. All three of us going, wake up and all that type of stuff . . . And he woke up.'

Vayu
This jazz-rock act is officially, it says here, the loudest band to hit Mumbai. Mumbai, as if you didn't know, is the new name for Bombay. That's pretty much all we know about them.

Manowar
While other bands have squandered their time trying to write songs that sound different to each other, Manowar have focused themselves on more achievable goals like growing their hair, making sure the word 'steel' is in all their album titles, and turning their amplifiers up.

Murder Squad
Toronto's loudest band. We can't quite hear them from here, but we were won over by these glowing endorsements on the band's press release: first they are described as 'A Barrage on the Senses both Musically and Physically'; we are then tempted by the suggestion that 'It hurts, IT HURTS!!!' Just try to keep us away. Oh. They are.

Blue Cheer
Lester Bangs had this to say about Blue Cheer: 'What counts here is not whether Leigh Stephens birthed that macho grunt before Mark Farner (both stole it from Hendrix) but that Stephens' sub-sub-sub-sub-Hendrix

guitar overdubs stumbled around each other so ineptly they verged on a truly bracing atonality.' What he doesn't mention is that they were really, really loud.

Elad's Guitar Army
Hailing from Windsor, Michigan, EGA describe themselves as the world's loudest band. We're tempted to say, 'Who doesn't?'

Spiñal Tap
How could we forget the band who have earned a distinguished place in rock history as one of England's loudest bands? Nigel's amps used to go to eleven. Then other people caught on, so now – when he needs 'that little extra push over the cliff' – he turns them all the way up to infinity.

Eleven Rock Stars* and their Real Names

Marilyn Manson
Had she known how he would turn out, his mum would perhaps have gone for something a bit more . . . *edgy*. As it is she went with Brian Hugh Warner.

Sid Vicious
Depending on which source you believe, John Simon Ritchie or John Simon Beverly. We think it's the former. No relation to Shane Ritchie.

Cheryl Baker
The reassuringly *nice* one from Bucks Fizz balanced Eurovision bad girl Jay Aston in a kind of Lennon/McCartney symbiosis for the Brotherhood of Man generation. Her real name was Rita Crudgington.

Marti Caine
Not a rock star as such, but – come on – Linda Denise Crapper. We couldn't let that one pass.

Brian Eno
Brian Peter George St John Le Baptiste De La Salle Eno. A good old Suffolk name, although many people still believe it to be from the planet

*(ish)

Xenon. *Eno* was invented in the 1850s and today is one of the most popular global gastrointestinal remedies.

Larry Parnes
Not so much a rock star who changed his name so much as a pop manager who dispensed names that set the whole idea in motion. Vince Eager (Roy Taylor), Marty Wilde (Reg Smith/Reg Patterson) and Billy Fury (Ron Wycherly) were all rechristened by him.

Mad Professor
Neil Fraser. We think he made the right choice.

Fish
Derek Dick. Coincidentally, Yes bassist Chris Squire was nicknamed Fish, supposedly for his propensity for long baths on tour.

Steve Harley
His name's Steve Nice, and he changes it to Steve Harley? Surely Nice is nicer. Oh well.

Cozy Powell
Colin Flooks. 'Let There be Drums' – that was his hit.

Henry Rollins
Henry Garfield. Seems a bit of a pointless one, if you ask us.

The Eleven Hairiest Beasts in Rock

Manowar
A band desperate to make the record books on any basis. It has to be said that from a distance they look like something a cat choked up. A very big cat, mind . . .

ZZ Top
Unique for having the bulk of their hair growth below nostril level, ZZ get special mention for maximum quantity of hair on the minimum quantity of musicians.

Guns N' Roses
Making it on to the list purely on the strength of British-born hairball Slash, whose mattressful of hair masks a sweet little face. So his mum tells us – no one else has ever seen it. Passport control must be hilarious.

The Levellers
Young? White? Wealthy? Desperate to freak out your parents? Take a picture of The Levellers along to your next hairdressing appointment.

The Muppets
Dr Teeth only hires 'em hairy – and he means hairy *everywhere*.

Freddie Mercury
Zanzibar's finest. Starts out with the classic Rita Tushingham, then, just to prove his versatility, trades it in for a full Magnum. Chest fur unvarying over twenty-five fluffy years.

The Dubliners
The Dubliners have been operating for more than thirty years. They've spent most of that time growing hair, and it shows.

Kings of Leon
Almost disqualified on suspicion of irony. Reinstated on suspicion of hilarity.

Dave Stewart
Made up for his partner's wilful tonsure with some of the biggest hair outside of LA hair metal, which leads us to …

The giddy world of hair metal
There are so many contenders from this one tiny sliver of rock history that we decided to give them their own category. The winners should have been Vixen but they were docked one point for being girls, so the eventual victors, by a *hair*, if you will, were the dangerously backcombed Britney Fox.

Kiss
Knights in Satan's service? Knights in Vidal Sassoon's service, more like.

Eleven Examples of Bands in Fiction

There's something about pop groups in fiction that somehow doesn't ring true. The names are part of it – many writers known for their carefully researched verisimilitude in other matters tend to panic when it comes to christening their imaginary combos and come up with something obviously fake, like Starsailor.

A very few authors and screenwriters have managed to overcome this sedentary variant of stage fright and have created bands that are so *right* that we're disappointed they aren't real.

Various, *A Clockwork Orange*

In Anthony Burgess's dystopian thump-fest the anti-hero, Alex, peruses the chart run-down as posted behind a record shop's counter. Rendered accurately by the movie adaptation's set dresser, it lists The Blow Goes, Bread Brothers, Comic Strips, Cyclops, Goggly Gogol, The Humpers, The Legend, The Sharks, Johnny Zhivago and, of course, Heaven Seventeen.

Every one of these names holds a promise that leaves us wanting more. And what did we get? Beethoven. On a synthesizer. Played by a lady-man.

Various, *Snow Crash*

Neal Stephenson populates his novel with band names that sound just as silly as the real thing. It's easy to imagine slipping Blunt Force Trauma on to the Monsters of Rock bill without exciting suspicion. Similarly, Sushi K could pass for floppy-fringed young Oriental romantics. Fierce debate still rages within the *Elevens* office as to whether one of us booked Vitaly Chernobyl & the Meltdowns for his Student Union dance in the mid-1980s.

The Cass Carnaby Five, *Thunderbirds*

Paradise Peaks is not an American porn star; rather it's an alpine resort catering principally to the puppet trade. It was here that house band The Cass Carnaby Five had their radio broadcasts altered by a mad scientist who wished to sabotage military transport flights. Fortunately for Cass Carnaby and his little wooden cohorts, the fiercely posh but undeniably talented Lady Penelope was placed undercover by her pals in the Thunderbirds organization in order to thwart this evil plan and give Sophie Ellis Bextor fashion tips.

The Carrie Nations, *Beyond the Valley of the Dolls*

Admittedly terrible, but monstrously influential all-female combo featured in Russ Meyer's trash classic. Dolly Read played the lead singer, Kelly MacNamara. Better yet, Cynthia Myers, who portrayed the band's bass player, was (half) dressed as a Christmas tree for *Playboy*'s December 1968 issue.

The Grams, *Powder*

You would be forgiven for thinking that, with a heading like this, we were on course for a free and frank discussion of class-A drugs. We aren't. That's in another list.

Breaking Glass, *Breaking Glass*

Wonderful things happen in this film – for example, an argument about the mix at the band's first recording session gets resolved when someone accidentally breaks the mixing desk, miraculously improving the sound to everybody's satisfaction. Hazel O'Connor's character develops a predilection for dressing up as one of those space ladies that David Bowie was married to in *The Man Who Fell to Earth*, then it all gets a bit much for her and she goes off for a lie down. It's a wonderful story and very true to life.

The Rutles, *Rutland Weekend Television*
Both a parody of and an affectionate tribute to The Beatles. Although without doubt immensely influential on later creations such as Spinal Tap, Bad News and Oasis, with hindsight The Rutles disappoint as comedy. Cracking tunes, though.

Arthur Ewing and his Musical Mice, *Monty Python's Flying Circus*
Best known for his pioneering performance of 'The Bells of St Mary's', Arthur Ewing has influenced many artists with his signature sound of mallet on rodent.

The Commitments, *The Commitments*
The time-honoured 'let's do the show right here' story, The Commitments were given life in Roddy Doyle's classic novel. You know, the one with the van in it. Not *The Van*, the other one.

The Partridge Family, *The Partridge Family*
Not strictly partridges (we checked) nor technically a family. Definitely fictional, though.

Spinal Tap, *This is Spinal Tap*
Of course no discussion of fictional music groups, and certainly not this one, would be complete without a mention of the ultimate imaginary band. Recounting the group's odyssey from their humble beginnings in Squatney to their phoenix-like triumph in Japan, the Spinal Tap movie is an object lesson in exactly how rock is done.

Eleven F***ing Offensive Band Names

Fuck Off
Well, *somebody* had to try this one. Our extensive research reveals that this group's records were rarely, if ever, played by Wogan.

FFW
German act originally called Freaky Fucken Weirdos. Record company predictably require bowdlerization before release.

NTM
Immensely rude in French. NTM stands for *nique ta mère*. Look it up.

Foetus
Jim Thirlwell, a.k.a. Clint Ruin, chose, inexplicably, to insulate his talent from a wider audience with a near-infinite variety of unpleasantly foetus-themed names, including (but not limited to): Scraping Foetus off the Wheel, Foetus Interruptus, Foetus All-Nude Revue, You've Got Foetus on Your Breath, and Phillip Toss and his Foetus Vibrations. Foetus Uber Alles not included here, due to lack of umlaut.

The Pogues
A more radio-friendly rendering of the band's original name, Pogue Mahone (an Anglicization of the Gaelic expression '*póg ma thón*', meaning 'kiss my arse'). Now if we could only persuade Shane to *floss*.

The Nipple Erectors
Another Shane MacGowan production. Not as rude as they thought it was, really.

Moors Murderers
An act so keen to get on with shocking your mum that they didn't find time to write any actual songs. Chrissie Hynde went on to form the stupendously successful if ill-starred Pretenders. Steve Strange went on to be somewhat Welsh.

Napalm Death
Intended to cause offence, but for those of us who were not combatants in the Vietnam War the effect tends more towards the mildly depressing. Band-leader Bill Steer tried again with his next project, Carcass. Well, that's all the farm animals alienated, then.

Gaye Bykers on Acid
Grebo band The Bykers were inexplicably dropped from Virgin Records after the release of their groundbreaking *Drill Your Own Hole* LP, which of course came without the centre hole that allows a record to be placed on a deck. Lovely job, fellas.

The Slits
The Slits, like Hole after them, sought to remedy the perceived male dominance of rock by asserting their untrammelled female sexuality in

their very name. Slight overreaction, girls, we would suggest, as there aren't all that many male groups called Knob to counteract.

Throbbing Gristle

Well-nigh unlistenable, but we're sure their mums were very proud – and their name sort of makes you think of cocks, so in they go . . .

THANK YOU
FOR THE MUSIC

Eleven Great Vocal Tics

There are many great rock voices. But some singers are more than just singers. This elite have the capacity to trademark their talent with one single, wonderful noise . . .

The Michael Jackson 'Ow!'
The distilled sound of a young and perhaps slightly confused young man grabbing his crotch just a little too tightly and realizing it hurts.

The James Brown 'Aiieow!'
The Godfather of Soul's songs do have words in them, but most of the time James Brown sings in what can only be described as the key of grunt.

The Tom Jones 'Huh'
Ah, the green, green grass of groan. Often found to be accompanied by a shove of the groin, on closer inspection the Tom Jones trademark is actually Welsh for . . .

The Elvis 'Uh-huh'
If some people, like Whitney Houston, treat singing like vocal gymnastics, then Elvis performed what is best described as a vocal thrust. Deep and Southern, the double-syllable drawl leaves no doubt that Elvis would have liked a little less on the conversation front and a little more on the action.

The Johnny Rotten laugh
'Right,' says Johnny at the start of 'Anarchy in the UK', and then there it is: 'Ha ha ha ha . . .' As laughs go, it's got a safety-pin through it.

The Bee Gees' 'Ha!'
Gibberish, to give it its technical name.

The Axl Rose scream
A thin white line of a sound: vocal feedback that gave Slash's squalling guitar a run for its money.

The Britney Spears 'Ow'
Lower than Jacko's, and several crotchets more suggestive thanks to its teenage twang, the 'Ow' is the noise of a Britney no more a girl, though conversely not yet a woman.

The Barry White 'Hmm'
We don't know what noises normal walruses make, but the love variety go low – so low, in fact, that a too-loud 'Hmm' from Barry can cause the floor to vibrate or a filling to loosen. The story of women sitting on speakers blasting out a bit of Barry is, sadly, as far as we're aware, apocryphal.

The Anastacia throat-clear
With lungs this big, you want to make sure there's no phlegm down there before you start singing. 'Woah-woah. Urr. Arrggh,' and so forth. Nice.

The Robert Plant banshee howl
With a wail as long as his hair, as lethal as John Bonham after a night on the everything, the banshee howl is, if anything, the musical equivalent of a red snapper receiving its last rites.

Eleven Great Pronunciations

Some singers accentuate the positive. Others accentuate the negative . . .

'Sunshine' by Liam Gallagher
'Cigarettes and Alcohol' is Oasis's signature song and there's no holding back from Liam in the pronunciation department. Firstly, there's the setting-out-the-stall opening-line adaptation of 'imagination' into 'imaginasheyun'. And then, instead of 'sunshine', there's 'sun-she-yine'.

'Fade' by Roger Daltrey
'My Generation' tackled that age-old rock problem of how to fit swearing into a song and still get it played on the radio. The Who's idea was the cunning use of the 'stutter'. They may have told everyone to 'f-f-f-ade away', but we all knew what they really meant.

'Vacant' by Johnny Rotten
No one pronounces with quite the venom of Johnny Rotten. His finest moment was on 'Pretty Vacant', in which he offers up the punk (rather than the mod) way to swear. Apparently all you need to do is find a word

with an expletive already inside, and yell that section of word like there's no tomorrow. For 'vacant', read 'vay-CUNT'. Fucking genius.

'Ziggy' by David Bowie
If you're ever called upon to do a David Bowie impression, smattering your singing with 'Zigg-ay's can work wonders for authenticity.

'Shout' by Tears for Fears
How can you pronounce 'shout' differently? The answer is to cunningly overlap the last line of the verse and first line of the chorus. One person sings 'jump', as in 'for joy', and the other person sings 'shout', as in letting it all out. The result? 'Shump.'

'Crucial' by Prince
'Crucial' is an essential part of the soul-ballad vocabulary, no more so than on Prince's 'Adore'. Prince describes his condition as 'crucial' and then just to emphasize the point, lets rip with a repeat, elongating the double syllable into a 'this love is real' six-pack. '*C-ru-sh-a-a-l.*'

'Angel' by Brett Anderson
As children we are always told off for dropping our aitches: ''oliday', ''appy birthday', ''Ello, Cleveland'. Suede's Brett Anderson made a sterling attempt to redress the balance on the early swoonsome ballad 'Sleeping Pills', throughout which Brett's beloved 'angel' becomes his, well, 'hangel'. Hamazing.

'Pump' by Technotronic
There are two ways in which one can say 'pump'. There's the posh way – 'parmp' – and the less so – 'pughmp'. In 1989, Technotronic added a third, Belgian alternative. Think 'porn' and change the 'n' to an 'mp'. 'Pormp.'

'Touch' by Phil Collins
It's the mid-eighties, and Phil and Genesis are penning the words to their Top Ten hit 'Invisible Touch'. Problem is, the title leaves the opening line to the chorus one syllable short. Here's the answer: add the word 'it'. 'Touch-it.' Is that the first word to the next line, in a sort of pre-echo way? Nope, the next word's actually 'she'. And not only that but also, the way Phil sings it, 'touch-it' sounds unerringly close to 'tough shit'.

'Apricot' by Carly Simon
Forget all that palaver about who 'You're So Vain' is about. The real mystery of the song is why Carly Simon pronounces 'apricot' as 'appricot'.

'Door' by Axl Rose
When Guns N' Roses knocked up their cover of 'Knocking on Heaven's Door', Axl came over all C&W. Goodbye, single-syllable 'door'. Hello, elongated-replacement 'dour-whore'. Maybe backstage entertainments weren't what they used to be.

Eleven Great Meaningless Words and Phrases

There are, of course, many great lyric writers in the world. But sometimes, as the great Irish philosopher Ronan Keating once commented, things are best said by in fact saying nothing at all.

'Oh a! Oh a!' from 'Video Killed the Radio Star'
This single might have earned Buggles a place in musical history as the first act to feature on MTV, but its finest moment is when the backing singer does her best Sandra Dickinson impression.

'De do do do de da da da' from 'De Do Do Do De Da Da Da'
I guess Sting just had less to say when he was in The Police. No '"Save the rainforest," is all I've got to say to you'. Just a couple of 'de's, a trio of 'do's and a 'da da da'. Which reminds us . . .

'Aha' from 'Da Da Da'
Two examples of 'da da da' in one Eleven would be greedy, but no matter: the German trio Trio have another gorgeous non-word up their sleeve. Part Arnie, part Alan Partridge, the 'aha' that ends each line is pure pop poetry.

'Woo-hoo!' from 'Song 2'
For all Damon Albarn's clever way with words on *Parklife* and *The Great Escape*, it wasn't until this, the second song from the eponymous fifth album, that Blur made waves overseas.

'Da diddly qua qua' from 'Stand and Deliver'
Adam Ant is the true master of the meaningless phrase with this gorgeous line, part Latin, part Bo Diddley's father.

'Zigazig-ha!' from 'Wannabe'
How precisely does one zigazig-ha? Maybe it's a cunning linguistic device

that, like some sort of lyrical chameleon, changes its meaning according to circumstance. So, to begin with, 'zigazig-ha' meant 'to become famous', whereas now it means 'to resurrect our careers from the ashes of our failed solo albums'.

'Ta na na na' from 'The Reflex'
The only bit from the Duran Duran number one that makes sense.

'Wooh wooh' from 'Elevation'
Bono's sitting-on-a-pin shout out showing that, for all the band's love of irony, U2 could still do dumb rock as well as anyone else.

'A-wop-bop-a-loo-lop a-lop-bam-boo' from 'Tutti Frutti'
Little Richard. Big impact.

'My-yi-yi-ow-woo!' from 'My Sharona'
The knack is all in the timing, the way the 'my' and the 'yi's cling on, loiter around for all they are worth and drag against the tune – and then there's that 'woo!' to kick things off again.

'Awwwwww!' from 'Le Freak'
Chic meaningless, meaningless chic. If Pavlov's Dog was a dancer, this would be the noise that would get him on his hind legs and boogying.

Eleven Songs You Should Never Play in a Guitar Shop

The moment you try out a guitar in a guitar shop is never an easy one. You're among peers, you want to impress – or more particularly, you don't want to look stupid. So, when the pony-tailed assistant with the Santana T-shirt passes you the Les Paul and says, 'Feel the action on this,' what soaring riff are you going to knock him out with?

'Stairway to Heaven'
In the film *Wayne's World*, Wayne faces such a situation when he notices a sign on the wall banning 'Stairway to Heaven'. The ban still stands, guys.

'Smoke on the Water'
Don't even think about it.

'Smells Like Teen Spirit'
A 'Smoke on the Water' for the nineties. Not only that, but the assistant will floor you with some comment about how it's just a rip-off of 'More than a Feeling' by Boston. If you're really unlucky, he might play you 'More than a Feeling' by Boston.

'House of the Rising Sun'
He'll think you're a busker.

'Wonderwall'
He might think you're a busker. Or you might just get a long lecture about how much better The Beatles were.

'Glad to be Gay'
The guitar shop is not an enlightened place.

'Anarchy in the UK'
Be careful. Although the world loved punk for what it was, for the guitar sales assistant there remains the nagging doubt that punks were a bunch of no-hopers who couldn't play their instruments.

'Wild Thing'
At which the assistant will have a flashback from the bad acid trip he had at Monterey in 1967, when he watched Jimi Hendrix play the song and set fire to his guitar. By the time you get to the end of the first line, the sprinklers will be on.

'Sultans of Swing'
For about thirty seconds in 1979, you could almost have got away with this. But, given that the assistant is likely to know it by heart, play it only if you know every last sodding note. Otherwise he's just going to pick you up on the smallest thing: 'I think you'll find that Mark hammers on the G in the rising arpeggio . . .'

Anything jazzy
He'll think you're a prat. Or, worse, Jamiroquai.

'Ziggy Stardust'
Before you know it, the assistant will be dropping to his knees and simulating giving you fellatio in front of a startled group of onlookers.

The Eleven Worst Lyrical Ideas

Sometimes, it's all about the music.

'Is There Something I Should Know' by Duran Duran
It was the eighties. People were worried about the bomb. That's the only reason we can come up with for the peerless metaphor Simon Le Bon slips out. According to Simes, guessing the name of the person in question is pretty much as 'easy' as (you won't get it if you don't know it) a 'nuclear war'.

'Rhythm Is a Dancer' by Snap
What can Snap think of to rhyme with dancer? Chancer? Prancer? Hang on a second, what about *cancer*? Yes! What about saying that rhythm is as 'serious' as 'cancer'? That'll sit nicely in an upbeat cheery dance hit . . .

'Maybe, Maybe' by A-ha
Ruminating on the end of an affair, Morten considers just exactly when it was that his relationship was no more. Perhaps it was 'over', he contemplates, when said missus threw him 'from the Rover'. We're not great readers of romance, but yes, Morten, we'd say it probably was.

'Ironic' by Alanis Morissette
What is irony? Is it 10,000 spoons when all you want is a knife? No, Alanis, it's not. Is it rain (pronounced 'rain', not 'ray-ee-yain') when you get married? No, again that's just a bummer. A pardon for someone who's just been sent to the chair? That's not irony; that's a badly managed judicial system in serious need of an overhaul.

'Wiggle Wiggle' by Bob Dylan
By employing the word 'wiggle' Bob finds himself in the esteemed company of well, only 2 in a Room. But, while their hit 'Wiggle It' might have been awful, at least it made sense. At least they didn't follow the title with the words 'like', 'a', 'bowl', 'of' and 'soup'.

'Savoir Faire' by Suede
We're not saying that Brett was short of ideas, but he was singing about a girl who lived 'in a house' – not only that, but she was also as 'stupid' as (you might get this) 'a mouse'.

'I Owe You Nothing' by Bros
With only a modicum of bitterness, Matt recounts watching his ex

'crumble'. Crumble like, well, Matt is pretty specific here. Not like a wall. Not like an old wall. But like a '*very* old wall'.

'I Won't Let the Sun Go Down on Me' by Nik Kershaw

Nik falls into that dangerous trap of not actually thinking a lyric through before singing it. Is he really going to avoid the sun going down on him? There's only one way he can do that, and that's by jumping on a plane and following the sun as it goes round the globe giving different countries daylight. The prohibitive cost of aviation fuel aside, the constant daylight is going to play serious havoc with his sleeping patterns. Nik, is that *really* what you want?

'Iron Hand' by Dire Straits

When writing this sentimental song about the miners' strike, Mark Knopfler obviously got all emotional: to describe the 'scene' of the battle between miners and police, the only rhyme he could come up with was that it shocked – can you guess? – 'the queen'.

'Mediate' by INXS

Usually, though not always, rhymes come in pairs: couplets, to give them their technical term. But why go to the bother of thinking of lots of different rhymes when you can use the same word-ending for the whole song? On 'Mediate', that's exactly what INXS did. Clever old Hutch rhymed '-ate' a whopping eighty-seven times. Words like 'fabricate'. And 'alleviate'. And 'segregate'. Exterminate?

'Instinction' by Spandau Ballet

Lyric-writing can be tricky sometimes. But, for those lyrically-lesser mortals, there is another solution. If your vocabulary is not suitably voluminous, then *simply make up a word*. That's what Spandau Ballet did, for their 1983 hit 'Instinction'. It *sounds* like it ought to be a word, doesn't it? But, oh no, it's nothing of the sort. What must Tony Hadley's English teacher have been thinking?

Pure insania.

Eleven Songs Containing Literary References

The poncey end of pop now, from various people who passed their English A level.

'Don't Stand So Close to Me' by The Police (Vladimir Nabokov)
Sting, fourth-dimensional human being, used all his huge knowledge to get in this not-remotely-pretentious reference in an otherwise taut, tight, early Police classic about teacher-pupil relations.

'Hey Jack Kerouac' by 10,000 Maniacs (Jack Kerouac)
The 10,000 Maniacs, who were neither 10,000 in number nor, indeed, Maniacs, focused on king beatnik and all-round On the Roadie on their breakthrough album, *In My Tribe*.

'Desolation Row' by Bob Dylan (Ezra Pound)
In 'Desolation Row', the whopping nine-minute, twelve-verse closer to *Highway 61 Revisited*, there isn't much, frankly, that Bob doesn't reference.

'Killing an Arab' by The Cure (Albert Camus)
Robert Smith took his inspiration from Camus' existential classic *L'Etranger*. We would have thought that was obvious, but apparently it wasn't to the British government. In 1991, 'Killing an Arab' joined the lengthy list of songs that were banned from the radio during the Gulf War.

'Run Baby Run' by Sheryl Crow (Aldous Huxley)
The song's heroine, we are told, is born in November 1963, on the day that Aldous Huxley died. Of course, Huxley died on the same day as J.F.K , and by defining the day in Huxley rather than J.F.K. terms, Sheryl is saying, 'Hey! Art is more important than politics! Neat, huh?' This blurring of views between the character and the songwriter confused some listeners: every year Sheryl gets cards from fans who assume her birthday is in November (it's actually in February).

'Country House' by Blur (Honoré de Balzac)
Summer 1995 and, at the height of Britpop, Blur showed their literary range by referencing both *Jackanory* and Balzac in one song. What Oasis made of Balzac is unclear – maybe they thought it was a bag to keep your footy gear in.

'Sylvia Plath' by Ryan Adams (Sylvia Plath)
The quietest moment on Ryan Adams' rollicking album *Gold*. There's a line about having a bath, because that rhymes, and another about having a laugh, even though she didn't very much.

'Shakespeare's Way with Words' by One True Voice (William Shakespeare)
One True Voice, you'll be pleased to have forgotten, were the *Popstars* boy-band rivals to Girls Aloud. The gist of the lyrics was that the boys

wished they had, as the title suggests, Shakespeare's way with words. 'To Be or Not to Be' might have been more appropriate.

'A Thousand Silver Spoons' by The Crash Test Dummies (T. S. Eliot)
This Canadian band had surprised everyone with their out-of-nowhere hit, 'Mmm Mmm Mmm Mmm'. Almost as if to prove that they could write songs containing more than one letter, the band went to literary lengths in the follow-up with this reference to modernist poet T. S. Eliot. It didn't sell.

'Obsessions' by Suede (Bret Easton Ellis)
The second single off the fifth album by Suede (the one that no one bought), 'Obsessions' was a suitably slinky slice of *Coming Up*-era fun. Brett (Anderson) references Bret (Easton Ellis), a suitably glossy, shocking and perhaps hollow novelist.

'Cemetry Gates' by The Smiths (Keats, Yeats and Wilde)
Morrissey references not one (Keats), not two (Yeats) but three (Wilde) literary giants. Keats and Yeats are, apparently, on one side, while Morrissey is in the Oscar Wilde camp. Whatever could it all mean?

The Eleven Best Rock Words to Use in a Game of Scrabble

Sometimes, size matters.

'Spottieottidopalisions' (track title) by Outkast

'Superfunkycalifragisexy' (track title) by Prince

'Hyperbolicsyllabicsesquedalymystic' (track title) by Isaac Hayes

Decksanddrumsandrockandroll (album title) by the Propellerheads

Dubnobasswithmyheadman (album title) by Underworld

'Psychoalphadiscobetabioquadoloop' (track title) by Parliament

'Psychoticbumpschool' (track title) by Bootsy's Rubber Band

'Supergroovalisticprosifunkstication' (track title) by Parliament

'Anotherloverholenyohead' (track title) by Prince

Promentalashitbackwashipsychosisenema from 'Promentalashitbackwash-ipsychosisenema Squad' (track title) by Funkadelic

Llanfairpwllgwyngyllgogerychwyndrobwllantysiliogogogochocynygofod, from 'Llanfairpwllgwyngyllgogerychwyndrobwllantysiliogogogochocyny-gofod (In Space)' (track title) by The Super Furry Animals

The Eleven Songs that Will Get You the Best Value from the Pub Jukebox . . .

So, you're feeling flush. You've got a whole shiny pound to put into the pub jukebox, which gives you ten songs at ten pence each plus a bonus one absolutely free. How can you maximize your investment?

'All Around the World' by Oasis
You can start with this dreary chart-topper from the Britpoppers' third album, *Be Here Now*. 'All Around the World' may last only nine minutes and twenty seconds, but it has the added bonus of feeling like it goes on for ever.

'The Asphalt World' by Suede
Towards the end of *Dog Man Star* things were getting so dark and broody that the band decided to turn prog. Bloody great, though, every last drop of its nine minutes and twenty-five seconds. And it obviously got something out of the band's system, because after that it was pop tunes all the way.

'Fool's Gold' by The Stone Roses
At nine minutes and fifty-three seconds, this stands just seven seconds short of a timeless ten minutes, but will be the one song in your eleven that will get you nods from everyone in the pub for making such a good choice.

'Stone to the Bone' by James Brown
The Godfather of Soul in scintillating early seventies form; grooving it like a bastard for nine minutes and fifty-seven seconds.

'Come Together' by Primal Scream
The classic *Screamadelica* cut of 'Come Together' takes a while to come

together, but, by the end of its ten minutes and twenty-one seconds, everything is all right with the world, you're loaded, movin' on up and higher than the sun all in one go.

'Marquee Moon' by Television
If it wouldn't seem like we were cheating, we'd suggest you put this song on twice because it's just so good. Ten minutes and forty seconds isn't enough for its two-pronged guitar attack that is often imitated, never bettered.

'The Look of Love' by Isaac Hayes
When it comes to Isaac, love takes what can only be described as a long look. A very long look. For an all-but-perfect (as far as we're concerned) eleven minutes and eleven seconds.

'Desolation Row' by Bob Dylan
The ten verses of the gorgeous closing song on *Highway 61 Revisited* veer from Einstein to Robin Hood, Bette Davis to Nero. Even better, you get a stonking eleven minutes and twenty-three seconds for your money.

'Shine On You Crazy Diamond (Part One)' by Pink Floyd
Back to the seventies now, and the song that makes up a good whack of the *Wish You Were Here* album. Celebrate the Floyd's tribute to Syd Barrett and gain yourself another thirteen minutes and thirty seconds.

'Welcome to the Pleasuredome' by Frankie Goes to Hollywood
Not the edited-down single version but the full-fat album version, weighing in at a friendly thirteen minutes and thirty-eight seconds.

'Monolith' by The Beta Band
Best to play this one last, partly because it goes on a bit and partly because it meanders enough for other drinkers to enquire if the jukebox has developed a fault. But, if you can get a full play, this track will give you a mighty satisfying fifteen minutes and forty-nine seconds.

Grand total: two hours, five minutes and seven seconds, or a fantastic seventy-five seconds for every penny in the slot.

And the Eleven Songs that Will Get You the Worst Value from the Pub Jukebox

So, you're feeling flush. You've got a whole shiny pound to put into the pub jukebox, which gives you ten songs at ten pence each plus a bonus one absolutely free. You know the economics by now but how can you minimize your investment in the most profligate fashion possible?

'You Suffer' by Napalm Death
Admittedly not necessarily found on every pub jukebox, but this classic of grindcore metal came free with the friendly sounding *Grind Crusher* compilation and at a lengthy one second is, as far as we're aware, one of the shortest singles of all time. (See below for the other.)

'Mega Armageddon Death (Part Three)' by The Electro Hippies
The flip-side to the Napalm Death single, not exactly outstaying its welcome at an equally frugal one second.

'Ballad of Jimi Hendrix' by The Stormtroopers of Death
In their poignant tribute to the guitar legend, Anthrax off-shoot The Stormtroopers of Death (SOD, for short) chew over his legacy for a whopping four seconds.

'Short Attention Span' by The Fizzy Bangers
From the album *Look Ma No Talent*. Nineties US rock band The Fizzy Bangers put aside any attention-span concerns with this seven-second ditty.

'This is Stupid' by The Bloodhound Gang
A wonderful aperitif before the band's sensitive ballad 'A Lap Dance is So Much Better when the Stripper is Crying', 'This is Stupid' is, well, stupid, but only for ten seconds.

'Miracle Cure' by The Who
A rock-opera snippet. Pete Townshend barely has time to get his arm all the way round the windmill during the song's twelve seconds.

'17' by The Smashing Pumpkins
It does exactly what it says on the sleeve notes to *Adore*: '17' lasts a pleasing seventeen seconds.

'Festerday' by Carcass
Lovely title, lovely band. But don't worry if you don't like them – this one's around for only twenty-two seconds.

'Her Majesty' by The Beatles
Let's move away from metal for a moment and relive The Beatles' last-ever notes. At twenty-three seconds, the cheeky coda to *Abbey Road* finds the Fab Four not hanging around to start their solo careers.

'Avalanche Rock' by The Avalanches
Less an avalanche than a rumble. The Avalanches rock for all of twenty-three seconds.

'Short Songs' by The Dead Kennedys
A collection of short songs wouldn't be complete without 'Short Songs' by The Dead Kennedys, in which Jello Biafra repeats his liking for short songs thirteen times and then stops. How short is 'Short Songs'? Twenty-eight seconds.

Grand total: two minutes and twenty-eight seconds, or a pathetic one and a half seconds for every penny in the slot.

Eleven Songs that Start with a Sound Effect

You can come in with your guitar riff, of course. But, if you want to start your song with a bang, why not reach for that battered old copy of *BBC Sound Effects* and do it all a bit differently.

'Love is the Drug' by Roxy Music (walking across gravel)
Obviously this wouldn't work if the driveway was concrete. Fortunately Bryan Ferry's house had gravel at the front, so we can hear him walk across from one speaker to the other, get into the car and drive away. We would make a joke about it being his Byron Ferrari, but the *NME* did that in the mid-seventies and Bryan hasn't really spoken to them since. So we won't.

'Thriller' by Michael Jackson (the squeaky door)
Again, it could all have been so quietly different. A can of WD40 and you'd never have known Michael was there. If you're going to do

Hammer Horror soul, you might as well begin with a Hammer Horror sound effect. We'll leave you to decide which record ends with the sound of Michael's career being firmly shut.

'Hell's Bells' by AC/DC (the bells)
A slightly literal interpretation of the music that is to follow, but, several years before Bob Geldof and Band Aid came along, these were the original clanging chimes of doom. Particularly impressive because, as far as we're aware, their ten-second duration contains no innuendo whatsoever, which for AC/DC must be something of a record.

'It's Only Natural' by Crowded House (the kitchen sink)
Not actually the kitchen sink, but as good as. Crowded House run through the list of sound effects that (and we're only guessing here) were beaten by 'Quack Quack Oops' for the gig on DLT's *Give us a Break*. Full marks for having absolutely nothing to do with the succeeding song in any shape or form.

'Two Tribes' by Frankie Goes to Hollywood (the air raid siren)
Nuclear-war song, World War Two siren. Rumours that the effect was put in to warn DJs like Mike Read that a Frankie song was about to be played on the radio have been completely made up by us to finish this entry with a cheap joke.

'Money' by Pink Floyd (cash tills)
Many songs are said to contain the sound of cash tills ringing. Only one actually does. Good job that the Floyd wrote the song back in the seventies; a more contemporary succession of credit-card machines whirring would make a much less interesting beginning.

'Starfish and Coffee' by Prince (the alarm clock)
A helpful wake-up call for the listener, halfway through the second side of *Sign o' the Times*, possibly put in for those who had drifted off during the preceding seven-minute funk jam of 'It'.

'Down on the Farm' by Little Feat (the frog)
Late-seventies album from the swamp-funk outfit kicks off with the sound of a frog. Ribbit. The singer tells the frog to shut up. The frog doesn't. Again the singer tells the frog to shut up. Again, the frog doesn't. This keeps going until the music begins. Pointless but fun.

'Psychedelic Shack' by The Temptations (knocking on the door)
With slightly more manners than demonstrated in Michael Jackson's 'Thriller', The Temptations knock before entering their 'shack'.

Particularly disconcerting to the unsuspecting listener who thinks there's someone at *their* door and gets up to see who it is. By the time they get back, the song is in full funk.

'Blackbird' by The Beatles (the sound of birds)
Well, what else would you use to accompany 'Blackbird'?

'Girls on Film' by Duran Duran (the clicking of cameras)
Another obvious choice, perhaps, but none the worse for it.

Eleven Songs about Singers

What better inspiration for a musician than another musician?

'The Beatles and the Stones' by House of Love
Guy Chadwick remembers the better points of the sixties.

'How Do You Sleep?' by John Lennon
A not-so-fond look back at the Fab Four – a certain Mr McCartney in particular.

'Brian Wilson Said' by The Barenaked Ladies
A knowing nod to The Beach Boys maestro, all sandpits and sitting in bed feeling miserable.

'When Smokey Sings' by ABC
Mr Robinson's voice is, according to Martin Fry, like the sound of violins. Or it could be 'violence' – the pronunciation isn't quite clear.

'Nightshift' by The Commodores
Marvin Gaye and other classic soul legends suitably remembered. Inexplicably covered by Dexy's Midnight Runners for their comeback.

'Like Dylan in the Movies' by Belle and Sebastian
A pun on *Don't Look Back*, rather than an in-depth analysis as to why *Hearts of Fire* was so shit.

'Cast No Shadow' by Oasis
Rumours of Richard Ashcroft's vampiric tendencies are tackled head on.

'Shine On You Crazy Diamond' by Pink Floyd
Both Part One and Part Two are about former front-man Syd Barrett.

'Jackie Wilson Said' by Dexy's Midnight Runners
Not about Jocky Wilson, as *Top of the Pops* famously and mistakenly thought.

'Fish out of Water' by Roland Orzabal
Orzabal puts the boot into former Tears for Fears chum Curt Smith.

'Dr Robert' by The Beatles
Classic Beatles track premonitionally lauding the work of the mid-eighties Blow Monkeys front-man. We think.

HELLO, CLEVELAND

Sewer Rats with Guitars: Eleven Moments of Sex Pistols Anarchy

They were anarchists and they didn't care. Apparently. Goodness me, if only Busted had been managed by Malcolm McLaren.

17 September 1976, Chelmsford Top-Security Prison
The Pistols entertained 500 or so persons detained at Her Majesty's pleasure. Paul Cook turned up drunk and proceeded to fall off his drum stool. Gosh – how rock 'n' roll! Things could only get better . . .

20 September 1976, 100 Club, London
During The Damned's set, Sid Vicious (who at this point was still a member of Siouxsie and the Banshees) threw a glass at the stage. It hit a pillar, broke and cut several people, among them one girl who got a glass splinter in the eye.

12 March 1977, Speakeasy Club, London
The Pistols got involved in a skirmish with one of the most influential DJs of the time. 'Whispering' Bob Harris, presenter of BBC2's *Old Grey Whistle Test*, was injured in the fracas and one of his engineers needed fourteen stitches in his head.

7 June 1977, the River Thames, London
Virgin Records and The Pistols played 'God Save the Queen' to celebrate Jubilee year on a boat on the Thames but dozens of police were waiting to meet them when they docked. The band were hurried away, but Malcolm McLaren and several others were arrested.

30 June 1977, Stockholm airport, Sweden
The most shocking Sid Vicious incident ever involved him spotting his heroines, Abba's Agnetha and Anni-Frid, at the airport, approaching them coyly and asking for their autographs. They screamed and ran away. Just think what we missed . . . Anarchy in, er, Sweden? Holidays in the snow?

8 July 1977, Randy's Rodeo Ballroom, San Antonio, USA
Vicious helpfully told the crowd: 'You cowboys are all a bunch of fucking faggots!' When a young cowboy tried physical retaliation, Vicious hit him with his bass. The cowboy later denounced The Pistols as 'sewer rats with guitars'.

9 July 1977, Kingfisher Club, Louisiana, USA
During the show Vicious started to have sex with a girl who got on stage. Afterwards the band argued so much that Steve Jones later refused to travel on the tour bus, so he and Cook flew to the remaining shows. Happily Buddy Holly wasn't around to offer them a lift.

10 July 1977, Longhorn Ballroom, Dallas, USA
Vicious scrawled the words 'I need a fix' in magic-marker on his naked chest; when a girl later headbutted him on the nose, he let the blood flow down his torso – causing Rotten to remark, 'Look at that: a living circus.'

25 December 1977, Ivanhoe Club, Huddersfield
Possibly the most notorious gig of all time. The Pistols played an afternoon Christmas party for children of local firemen, laid-off workers and single-parents. 1,000 bottles of pop and a huge cake were supplied by Virgin, who also laid on free buses. Rotten dived head-first into the cake and a food-fight ensued.

21 June 1996, Hollola Festival, Sweden
Rotten shouted, 'I can't hear you,' at the 15,000-strong audience, who responded by throwing beer and plastic bottles at the group. Rotten, perhaps worried about his dry-cleaning bill, then yelled, 'Stop, stop, stop! We can go home now, you know – we've already been paid.'

Late February 1979, Heathrow airport, London
It is rumoured that, after Vicious's death while on bail for murder, his mother dropped the urn containing his ashes at Heathrow airport and Sid got sucked up into the air-con. This prompted Rotten to say, in 1996, 'The only way we can reform properly is if we get a fucking hoover to bring Sid back.'

On that bombshell we wanted to know what the world of rock thought of The Sex Pistols. Hmm . . .

EMI press release, 7 December 1976
'We shall do everything we can to restrain their public behaviour, although this is a matter over which we have no real control.'

Pete Townshend
'*Never Mind the Bollocks* is one of the greatest records of the twentieth century.'

Sir Cliff Richard
'The Sex Pistols were the worst thing ever to happen to rock 'n' roll.'

Kurt Cobain
'Johnny Rotten was the one I identified with – he was the sensitive one.'

Noel Gallagher
'You could put together a *Best of . . .* from The Clash's five albums and it wouldn't be worth a wank next to *Never Mind the Bollocks*.'

Billy Joe Armstrong, Green Day
'The Sex Pistols suck; we're more punk than they ever were.'

Johnny Rotten at the 100 Club press conference, 18 March 1996, on the eve of the reformed Pistols' Filthy Lucre tour
'We are not trying to bring the monarchy down any more. Our very good fifth member, Lady Di, is doing an excellent job. We offered to do a benefit for her because she needs the cash.'

'I'm worried about the geriatric fans who will turn up – I hope it rains and they get their wheelchairs stuck in the mud.'

'Sid was nothing more than a coat-hanger to fill an empty space on stage.'

'We won't bother rehearsing – you know the songs as well as we do. I bet you play them better as well.'

And, er . . .

Avril Lavigne
'I'm like a Sid Vicious for a new generation.'

Eleven People Bono Called Live from the Stage During the Zoo TV Tour

For the finale of each show during the 1992–1993 Zoo TV world tour, Bono wore a gold suit, devil's horns and white face-paint. Calling himself Mister Macphisto, the Last Rock Star, he made live phone calls from the stage.

Bill Carter in Sarajevo
Bono dialled an American named Bill Carter in Sarajevo for an update on the situation. 'People are starving because there's no food?' Bono repeated, and asked Carter if Bosnia felt betrayed by the West. 'Bill, I just want to say one thing: we are ashamed to be European.'

Detroit Speedy Pizza
'Is this Speedy Pizza? I'd like to order 10,000 pizzas for Detroit. We're at the Palace. I *am* serious. I'm very serious. You can't make 10,000? Just make as many as you can. OK. What? My name is Bono.' Sure enough, a guy arrived with a huge trolley of pizzas and went into the crowd to 'distribute' them. The crowd descended on him and a tidal wave of pizza boxes shot up into the air.

George Bush Snr at the White House
The White House operator couldn't get the President on the phone. 'You mean George is the President and he goes to bed before two a.m.? Tell him to watch more television,' Bono said and hung up. 'I guess I'm just not as important as I thought I was,' he added to the crowd.

Allesandra Mussolini
In Italy he told Benito Mussolini's niece that she was 'doing a great job filling the old man's boots'!

A travel agent in Rotterdam
Bono spoke to a very cheerful woman called Monique: 'I am looking to leave Amsterdam tonight, and I'd like a flight out of Schiphol this evening.' After some banter she offered him a flight to Singapore the next morning. He then sang her a song. Nice.

Queen Beatrix of the Netherlands
'Shall we give her a call to find out whether she is into rock 'n' roll or not?' Bono screamed at the crowd. But the royal receptionist did not appreciate the joke and hung up. 'Well now,' Bono blurted out, 'the last time royalty hung up on me I sent the House of Windsor up in flames!'

The Pope
He suggested that the Pope should do a world tour, then picked up the phone, saying, 'Let's see if we can wake the good fellow up.' He couldn't get through.

Akebono
He called the world-champion sumo wrestler and challenged him to an arm-wrestling contest at the Tokyo Dome.

Salman Rushdie
From Wembley Arena he called Rushdie, who, because of an Iranian edict calling for his death, had been in hiding since 1988. Rushdie was actually backstage, ready to accept the call; he then walked on stage to a standing ovation.

Luciano Pavarotti
Bono sang 'I Just Called to Say I Love You' down the line to him.

George Bush Snr at the White House
Bono said to the crowd, 'Let's call George one last time, waddaya say?' Then, on the phone, 'Hello, is that the White House? What? George isn't available? But it's our last night! Can I leave a message for George? Hello? I just wanna say I won't be bothering him any more from now on. I'm gonna be bothering Bill Clinton now . . .'

Nowadays, of course, all these people probably call *him*.

Eleven Live-and-Kicking Bootlegs

Here are eleven to search for on the Net before you sit back smugly in the knowledge that it is illegal to sell them but not, curiously, to buy them.

Liver Than You'll Ever Be, **The Rolling Stones**
This recording of the 1969 Oakland Colosseum concert gets the most votes as it prompted Decca to release *Get Yer Ya Ya's Out* some two months later, even lifting *Liver*'s 'Little Queenie' for the album. However, we are also intrigued and tickled by the possibilities of the cheekily titled *Blind Date Revisited* two-CD set from Toronto, May 1979 – the first CD contains a benefit for a blind-audience show given by Keith Richards and the New Barbarians as part of his community service for a drug conviction. Not a sign of Cilla Black.

The Complete Hollywood Bowl Concerts 1964/1965, **The Beatles**
There are literally hundreds of bootlegs, including the gorgeously titled *Jelly Beans Hailing in a Dreamlike Noise* CD from the Empire Theatre,

Liverpool, in 1963, but the one we've plumped for includes all three of the relevant concerts as well as press conferences and radio interviews and some genuinely never-before-heard stereo tracks. It even comes with a very informative booklet . . . allegedly.

Free Trade Hall in Manchester, Bob Dylan
They don't come more legendary than this 1966 recording. It features the infamous cry of 'Judas' and is generally acknowledged as one of the first bootleg CDs, having been given the digital treatment in the late 1980s. It was finally put out on official release in 1998 but the original bootleg still has enormous monetary and show-off value.

Filmore East/Live in New York, The Who
This 1966 recording captures The Who making the transition from English pop-art band to the more experimental and hard-rock sound that led to *Tommy* and one of the most explosive rock 'n' roll bands of the seventies. Rock on.

Keep Smiling, Brian Wilson
Although *Smile* – the great unfinished studio album – has been the begetter of countless bootlegged versions, the real bootleg to own is this one, of the Royal Festival Hall World Premiere in February 2004. Unfortunately, it being an audio-only recording, it misses the classic moment when Brian has to check his autocue to see which word comes after 'Barbara' in the track 'Barbara Ann'! There are also hundreds of Beach Boys live bootlegs and the best one, by title alone, has to be *Mike Love Not War* from the 1966 Michigan State University gig.

Dick's Picks: Volume 8, The Grateful Dead
They played approximately 100 to 150 shows per year from 1967 to 1995 and actively encouraged the 'Deadheads' to tape them, so one is completely spoilt for choice when it comes to finding The Grateful Dead's best bootleg. That said, this recording comes up time and time again and features the 2 May 1970 Harpur College gig. Man.

Destroyer: The Swinging Pig, Led Zeppelin
This mixing-desk tape from the 1977 Richfield Coliseum gig in Cleveland was sneakily transferred to CD and became a six-disc set featuring two complete shows from consecutive nights. Get out the Led.

David Bowie with Lou Reed, David Bowie
Although some diehards will cite the 1976 *Resurrection on 84th Street* recording, taken as being Bowie at his peak, we rather like the sound of this recording of Dave with Lou Reed from their May 1972 Kingston

Polytechnic gig and the Royal Festival Hall gig two months later. This was Reed's first-ever live performance in Europe! Go for the Japanese release if you can find it.

All Those Years, Bruce Springsteen
Bootlegs of The Boss's live shows, unreleased studio tracks and outtakes are charmingly called 'BruceLegs' and more than 100 new ones surfaced in 2003 alone. This multi-CD release celebrating the first ten years of touring is widely believed to be better than the official live boxed set. But we suspect that this debate is born to run and run . . .

17 Nussbaum Road, 1st Experience, Nirvana
In January 2004 a bootleg was issued of the first-ever live show Nirvana played. It was recorded at a house party at Nussbaum Road, Raymond, W.A., and includes two songs that have still never been officially released. The quality isn't particularly great, but it's history so just live with it. Worth buying just for track thirteen, 'Pre-Mexican Seafood Noise'. OK?

The Great Gig in the Sky, Pink Floyd
This Empire Theatre recording from 16 November 1974 is hilarious because you can hear the bootlegger chatting to the guy next to him during breaks between songs, then, when Floyd start a new number, getting rather cross and saying, 'No talking, I'm taping right now!'

Just Give Us the F***ing Money: Eleven Live Aid Memories

Live Aid featured 60 of the world's biggest rock stars and was held simultaneously over a 16-hour period in 2 different countries in front of a live audience of 162,000 and broadcast to an estimated 1.9 billion TV viewers in 150 countries across the world. Everyone has their own memories from that day and here are just eleven of ours . . .

Phil Collins, time traveller
Phil played with a re-formed Led Zeppelin at Wembley, then jumped on Concorde, jetted across the Atlantic and duetted with Sting and played again as a solo artist in Philadelphia later in the same day . . . 'I was in England this afternoon . . . Funny old world, innit!'

Elvis lives
For all the stadium posturing and larger-than-life performances, it was the simplicity of Elvis Costello's rendition of 'All You Need is Love' that sticks in many minds.

Got back – almost
No Fab Three, alas, but we did see a re-formed Status Quo (who opened the concert with the rabble-rousing anthem 'Rocking All Over the World'), Black Sabbath back with Ozzy, and, of course, The Who. Pete Townshend said, 'We always said we'd never play together again. We always meant it. But it would have been kind of difficult not to get together again for this day.'

May I have the next dance?
U2, having just completed a nine-month tour, played an amazing set and Live Aid was a turning point for them. They became kings of stadium rock 'n' roll and in the midst of their breathtaking performance Bono grabbed a girl from the crowd and danced with her in front of almost two billion people.

Queen of all they surveyed
Bob Geldof is not alone in thinking that it was the boys from Queen who stole the show. Their set became a singalong and Freddie, dressed in trademark white jeans and white vest, swinging the mike stand back and forth, left the audience screaming for more.

Pure sex
Jagger duetted with Tina Turner and they came as close to having live sex on television as you can with your clothes on and that many people watching . . .

Bob Dylan trod in something nasty
After a frankly terrible, under-rehearsed set with Ronnie Wood and Keith Richards, the Bobster decided to announce that, 'It would be nice if some of this money went to the American farmers.' Er, right. Actually, this remark did instigate Farm Aid, which has raised millions over the years, but that's not really the point.

Saint Bob walked on water
After the event, Geldof said, 'My back had been hurting and Bowie had been giving me a massage before I went on . . . I walked on stage and the noise hit me . . . it was staggering . . . suddenly my back wasn't hurting as much.'

Macca's mike failed during 'Let It Be'

But it didn't matter – by then the whole world was singing along and Macca and Pete Townshend were carrying an exhausted Geldof on their shoulders and more than $70 million had been raised, all of which went to the charity. Macca's mike also failed at the finale of the Queen's Golden Jubilee Concert at Buckingham Palace in 2002. Same engineer? Lennon fan? We will never know.

Absentees

Michael Jackson would have been an obvious choice but didn't want to get involved. Bruce Springsteen was in the middle of an eighteen-month tour so couldn't make it happen and Prince had retired from live shows. One imagines that if the much-rumoured Live Aid II is ever to happen then at least two of these three will make up for their previous absenteeism. One may be otherwise engaged.

And, erm . . . Geldof's car went missing

Apparently, when Saint Bob left the stadium after the most successful day in charity history, he discovered that his car had gone missing; he then had to hitch-hike home. Quality.

Scream and Shout: Eleven Beatles Live Moments

Flaming Prophylactics

The Beatles (with Pete Sutcliffe on drums) were forced to leave Hamburg in 1963 for three reasons: firstly, because of a boring contract dispute, secondly, because George was found to be underage; and thirdly, because Paul and Pete tacked a condom to the wall of a club and set fire to it.

This is London

Their first-ever BBC appearance, on 3 August 1962, was on a programme called *Teenager's Turn (Here We Go)* and consisted of two songs: 'Memphis, Tennessee' and 'Please Mr Postman'. They also recorded 'Hello Little Girl' during the same session.

John, Paul, Ringo, George . . . and Rolf?

From Christmas Eve until New Year's Eve 1963, at the Astoria Theatre in London's Finsbury Park, they hosted their Christmas Show, which saw audiences being entertained by a mixture of sketches and songs from the likes of Billy J. Kramer, Cilla Black and the Barron Knights and was compered by 'Uncle' Rolf Harris.

Scream, shout and get your hair cut
The day after their debut show at the Colosseum, Washington D.C., on 11 February 1964, the US *Herald Tribune* described the Beatles phenomenon as '75% publicity, 20% haircuts and 5% cheerful mournings' and US President Lyndon B. Johnson told British Prime Minister Sir Alec Douglas-Home, 'I like your advance guard. But don't you think they need haircuts?'

John, Paul, George . . . and Jimmy?
When Ringo was hospitalized in London on the eve of The Beatles' 1964 Australian tour, drummer Jimmy Nicol was drafted in to make up the numbers. During the tour, every time one of The Beatles asked Jimmy how he was getting on, his reply was always the same: 'It's getting better.' Sounds like a cue for a song? The tour is also notable for a display of the famous Lennon dead-pan wit – at their first Australian press conference Paul was asked by one journo what he expected to find in Australia and John replied quickly, 'Australians.'

The ambassador speaks
In his report to London about The Beatles' 1966 sell-out Japanese tour (of thirty-minute concerts), the British ambassador said that 'as value for money this does not compare at all well with a whole-evening recital by Rubinstein which could be heard last week in Tokyo for the same price'. He ended with a slight note of caution: 'Our next Very Important Guests are The Rolling Stones.'

Back in the USA
On Monday 29 August 1966 at Candlestick Park in San Francisco they made their last-ever concert-tour appearance, to a crowd of 25,000 people and, for some reason, 17,250 empty seats. The set-list for the thirty-three-minute show was: 'Rock and Roll Music', 'She's a Woman', 'If I Needed Someone', 'Day Tripper', 'Baby's in Black', 'I Feel Fine', 'Yesterday', 'I Wanna Be Your Man', 'Nowhere Man', 'Paperback Writer' and 'Long Tall Sally' (encore); poignantly, the last notes played were by John, who strummed the opening bars of 'In My Life' as he left the stage.

All they needed was love
The John Lennon-composed song 'All You Need is Love' was specially commissioned by the BBC and broadcast live on *In Our World*, the first-

ever global TV programme, on 27 June 1967. The brief was to 'keep it simple so that viewers across the globe will understand'. Lennon did and 350 million people understood. Among those who sang the chorus were Marianne Faithfull, Jane Asher, Patti Boyd and some bloke called Mick Jagger. No sign of Rolf or Cilla, alas.

Up on the roof
The Beatles' last-ever live gig, on 30 January 1969, was played to an audience of pigeons and sound engineers and took place on the roof of the Apple offices in London's Savile Row. The police arrived forty-two minutes into the set, perhaps following complaints from local office workers, and forced an early ending to the show. Nobody was arrested – although, given that they knew the event was being captured on film, one wonders whether the Fabs were hoping they would be.

And then there were three
On 23 June 1994, Paul and Ringo joined George at his home to work on the documentary – *The Beatles Anthology*. They decided to film themselves recording several rock 'n' roll oldies and on 4 December 1996 a tantalizing one-minute clip of them playing 'Blue Moon of Kentucky' was broadcast on US television. We believe this to be the only public screening of The Beatles playing live since 1969.

And then there were two
In 2002, Eric Clapton brought together a stellar cast of musicians and friends, including Jeff Lynne, Tom Petty, Paul McCartney, Ringo Starr, Billy Preston, Joe Brown and Ravi Shankar, for a tribute entitled Concert for George at the Royal Albert Hall. The most tear-jerking moment of them all was their version of 'While My Guitar Gently Weeps'.
Fab!

No Evian, No Lilies, No Carnations: Eleven Unreasonable Demands

When a rock band hit pay-dirt and go on the road for their first major tour, greed and taking the piss take over. The more outrageous the 'must-have' requests for their backstage comfort, the better.

Are you cut out to be a promoter? Read on . . .

Oops, I called it again

Britney Spears needs a phone with an ex-directory number; any unauthorized calls made to the line will cost the promoter a cool $5,000 fine per call. And please don't forget her two boxes of Pop Tarts and 240 (read that again) full-sized cotton bath towels. The mind boggles.

Red hot

We can just about accept their need for the meditation room with an armless love-seat and two aromatherapy pillar candles, and we'll throw in the twelve Starbucks Frappuccinos and the small box of Lucky Charms for good measure, but can someone please explain the Red Hot Chili Peppers' need for six pairs of white crew sport socks ('sport logo OK'), four pairs of black cotton boxer shorts with button fly, Hawaiian mineral water ('absolutely no Evian') and an abundant supply of ice? Is there something we are missing out on?

They bring their own balls

The Stones need a full-size snooker table ('not a pool table') but please do relax in the curious knowledge that the 'tour will provide their own snooker balls'. And don't forget the five video-type games, to include: 'a motor or driving-type game, a pinball machine, a combat game, a virtual-reality game and a game suitable for families or small children'. Rock 'n' roll!

Coming up for air

ZZ Top must have oxygen and face masks available backstage thirty minutes prior to performance and there must be a 'medical doctor' available on call at all times. Two points here: firstly, how do you fit an oxygen mask over a beard? And secondly, it's good that they specified a 'medical' doctor. Imagine the scene otherwise – one of the ZZ people collapses and you summon a doctor of philosophy to discuss the meaning of life. Ouch.

Blink and you'll miss it

What do Blink-182 get up to backstage with a Polaroid camera, six bananas, a jar of crunchy peanut butter, a bottle of Echinacea and a large tray of sprouts? Don't ask, but do be nice to the cleaning staff afterwards.

A whiter shade of pale

J-Lo wants a white room, white tablecloths, white sofas, white roses, white lilies and white curtains – but, curiously, she will try to catch you out with the fact that she wants *green* grapes and some *yellow* roses with *red* trim. Got that? If she ever shares the bill with Pink, Blue, Al Green,

The Purple Gang, James Brown, Simply Red, Black Sabbath or David Gray there could be real problems.

Please don't bring me flowers any more

For Elton John's dressing room please provide one love-seat, four large green plants and a 'large arrangement of coloured flowers' (no chrysanthemums, lilies, carnations or daisies – you can give them to J-Lo). We hope you don't confuse a 'love-seat' with a 'love-swing' which, our sources tell us, is something very different indeed.

You can't hold a candle to them

The fragrant Destiny's Child are easy-to-accommodate guests – as promoters just bung them fresh ginger root (very important), two large strawberry candles, two bars of Dove soap, an ironing board, a jar of 'honeybee honey' and some wheat bread. Before you get lulled into a false sense of security, remember that all the foods must be served on 'fine china and dinnerware' and they also want a mere twenty-four towels. Next to Britney they seem a bit dirty, to be honest.

'Sharon!!'

Ozzy Osbourne requires the odd combination of an on-site ear, nose and throat doctor, who can administer him a B12 and anti-inflammatory shot, and 'ten 50-pound liquid high-pressure CO_2 syphon tanks'. Let's hope you don't get these items confused.

Carry on at your Convenience

TLC would like you to provide a toaster oven, a crock pot, a box of Throat Coat, an oxygen tank and three masks, a Euphoric Aveda candle, a box of Kleenex and one portable toilet for their exclusive use. The latter must be lockable, new or in perfect condition and positioned behind the stage. At the end of the performance it should be removed as soon as they've left the building.

3-2-1 You're back in the room

At the other end of the scale we discovered the contract rider for the Christopher Carter Hypnosis Show, which is extraordinary. Carter has the audacity to demand that the promoter provides 'a sound system that should have the capacity to play cassette tapes'.

Outrageous.

Eleven Festivals and Free Concerts

I am the god of hellfire and I bring you . . . er . . . wind
The most stirring memory of the 1968 Isle Of Wight Festival is not of the Jefferson Airplane light show projected on a sheet, nor of the gyrations of Marc Bolan. It is of the high crosswinds that scuppered Arthur 'The Crazy World of Arthur Brown' Brown's plans to arrive on stage from a hot-air balloon. The same wind later extinguished the flame on the top of his head during his signature number, 'Fire'. Worthy of Spiñal Tap.

Hello, money, my old friend
Simon and Garfunkel put aside years of acrimony on 19 September 1981, when they played a free concert to 500,000 people in NYC's Central Park. Of course, the notion of a 'free concert' alters slightly when you think of what they picked up from broadcast rights, merchandise, renewal of interest in their back catalogue, the subsequent live album and the CD repackaging, but it's the thought that counts. They are back again touring the world in 2004.

If I said you had a sandy body, would you hold it against me?
On New Year's Eve 1994, the people of Rio de Janeiro decided to hold a beach party on a little patch of sand they call Copacabana. They booked a singer called Rod Stewart and set up a stage for him and 3.5 million people turned up, to party, to sing 'I Am Sailing' and to marvel at his tartan trousers.

Don't touch the brown dial
In 1969, 450,000 people gridlocked the US getting to Woodstock, where they learnt how to take their clothes off, throw mud, enjoy free love, drop acid and smoke grass while listening to the likes of Joplin, Jefferson Airplane, The Who, The Band and Joan Baez. The sound system was so powerful that even when turned down to one it caused physical pain to anyone standing within ten feet of it. Just think what it could do when turned up to eleven . . .

The day the music died
In August 1997, 750,000 people turned up to the free concert in NYC's Central Park given by one of the world's biggest country-music stars, Garth Brooks (who he?), and special surprise guests Billy Joel and Don McLean. Highlights included Garth and Billy's 'New York State of Mind' duet and then being joined by Don to sing a little song about driving chevys to something called a levée (whatever that is) while being watched by good ole boys drinking whiskey and rye. *Newsday* compared the show to Disney's *Pocahontas*: 'a well-executed, if unchallenging, spectacle'. Priceless.

Oops, they did it again

The attempt to recreate the spirit of Woodstock thirty years on, in 1999, went horribly wrong. Musically it rocked, with a bill that ranged from Alanis Morissette to The Red Hot Chili Peppers, but, with ticket prices of $150, water selling at $4 a bottle, four rapes, countless arrests, fences being burnt down and rioting, it was the antithesis of peace and love.

Kill for a ticket

In December 1969, The Rolling Stones staged a free concert at Altamont Speedway outside San Francisco and hired the Hell's Angels to do the security (a bit like hiring Gary Glitter to run the crèche, we imagine). The mood at the show turned ugly early on, and escalated from there – culminating in the murder of Meredith Hunter by a Hell's Angels member. Three other people died that day as well: two were run over and one drowned. Some blamed the violence on the song 'Sympathy for the Devil' and The Stones did not play it in concert again for six years.

Mud, glorious mud

After the 2004 Glastonbury Festival in the UK the talk wasn't of Morrissey, Macca or Oasis but was of a small bag of mud that was sold by a festival-goer on eBay. There was no reserve but bidding started at an amusing 99p. The seller's description read: 'This should arrive nice and damp with early Glastonbury dew still soaking into it.' The owner collected the mud from in front of the Pyramid stage and it finally sold for an astonishing £490 (postage and packing included, luckily). Half the money (only half?!) went to charity.

And that's jazz

The opening night of the first Monterey Jazz Festival, in 1958, featured performances by Dave Brubeck and, just nine months before her death, Billie Holiday. The evening's highlight, however, came when Dizzy Gillespie welcomed his hero Louis Armstrong to the stage. Dizzy dropped to his knees and kissed Satchmo's hand in homage. They do things so nicely in the jazz world, don'tcha think? No headbutting, bottling or even mud.

That Yoko – she'll have the shirt off your back

The 14-Hour Technicolour Dream, held on 29 April 1967 at London's Alexandra Palace, was so spaced-out that no one can be sure of who actually played there – although Hendrix, the era-defining 'Granny Takes a Trip' band The Purple Gang and some blokes called Pink Floyd certainly made an impression. For one lucky girl, the most lasting impression was probably made by Yoko Ono, at whose suggestion she volunteered to have her clothes cut off gradually by members of the audience. Oh Yoko.

Rock around the track
This free concert at the Grand Prix auto circuit in Watkins Glen, NYC, was attended by 700,000 people and featured The Grateful Dead, who opened the gig by playing for a bladder-busting five hours. (Rumour has it that some of Jerry Garcia's guitar solos were so long that people grew beards during them.) The show is considered by some to be the greatest free heavy-metal concert of all time – though presumably not by the 137,000 people who mistakenly paid for their tickets . . .

Eleven of the Best Gigs Ever?

Your favourite gig memory might feature an unknown band in a filthy venue in the scummiest part of town or worshipping at an enormodome (with good car-parking) at the altar of a rock icon. In the world of musical appreciation one man's Celine Dion is truly someone else's Nirvana, but we could only choose eleven . . .

The Jimi Hendrix Experience at Finsbury Park Astoria, London, 31 March 1967
Hendrix was lying on the stage playing the guitar with his teeth when it suddenly burst into flames. You can't argue with that. Schmokin'.

Led Zeppelin at the Royal Albert Hall, London, 9 January 1970
When Led Zeppelin played a concert, it wasn't just a concert – it was an event. Our man in the leathers reports that this gig experience was truly breathtaking, and described Plant as looking like 'a caveman who appeared to be a ball of hair with eyes protruding'.

Nirvana at Reading Rock Festival, 30 August 1992
Their last-ever UK gig before Kurt met his maker. Didn't catch it live? Nevermind – it's all available on CD.

Pink Floyd's *The Wall* at Potsdamer Platz, Berlin, 21 July 1990
Roger Waters performed Pink Floyd's album to celebrate the removal of the real wall, with guests including The Scorpions, Bryan Adams and Van Morrison. But no Dave Gilmour. Obviously.

Prince at Hammersmith Apollo, London, 5 October 2002
He even invited audience members on stage to dance with him. The little angel.

Queen at Live Aid, Wembley Stadium, 13 July 1985
Enough said.

Radiohead at Glastonbury Festival, 28 July 1997
Radiohead's Saturday-night set in front of 40,000 mud-drenched fans was described by festival organizer Michael Eavis as the most inspiring festival gig in thirty years. That's good enough for us – he's seen everyone . . . even 'Uncle' Rolf Harris.

The Rolling Stones at London Astoria, 27 August 2003
The intimacy of the gig at this 2,000-seat theatre caused one fan to describe it as a 'unique precious jewel of a gig which completely satisfied the rhythm of every moment I've spent listening to their music in my life'.

U2's Popmart Tour at Wembley Arena, London, 22 and 23 August 1997
With its vast, almost dwarfing stage and wrap-around video backdrop, this edgy tour divided critics but delighted the fans.

Brian Wilson at the Royal Festival Hall, London, 20 February 2004
Sort of *Night of the Living Dead* on a surfboard.

Oasis at Knebworth, 11 August 1996
Noel Gallagher's opening remark was typical: 'This is history. This is history. Right here, right now, this is history.' Liam retorted: 'No it fooking isn't, yer daft twat – this is Knebworth.'
   And so it was.

'We Interrupt this Performance . . .': Eleven Moments when Rock Stopped Rolling

Another trip in the hall
A thousand people plunged to the floor on the opening night of the Pink Floyd Division Bell tour at Earl's Court when a section of seating collapsed.

Common person
Jarvis Cocker protested against 'the way Michael Jackson sees himself as some Christlike figure with the power of healing' by invading the stage

during Jacko's performance of 'The Earth Song' at the 1996 Brits. He was arrested but never charged. Jarvis, that is.

Lipstick, powder and paint
The Reverend Marilyn Manson – priest of the Church of Satan – walked on stage during a Nine Inch Nails concert at the Delta Center in Salt Lake City after having been banned from opening for them. He then proceeded to rip up a copy of *The Book of Mormon* and chuck the pages at the audience. A long hard road out of hell, indeed . . .

'Who do you want me to dedicate it to?'
In-store signings are not sedate if Green Day are in attendance. Their 1997 appearance at Tower Records in New York featured a forty-minute performance interspersed with drenching racks of CDs with beer and water, spraypainting 'FUCK YOU' on the inside of the store window and urging the fans to riot because 'it's your prerogative'.

Ice, ice, baby
Who can forget Chumbawamba's curiously named Danbert Nobacon pouring an entire bucket of ice over the Deputy Prime Minister John Prescott at the 17th Annual Brit Awards? As Danbert once said, 'Anarchism is the struggle to be human in an environment which encourages the inhuman.' Where does that leave Prescott?

Dip me in honey and throw me to the lesbians
If you are reading this in the US then the thought-police will probably come and get you. In 1998, the Irmo High School in Columbia decided to ban a special concert by the Indigo Girls because some parents were worried about the sexuality of the duo, Amy Ray and Emily Saliers. This started a trend and three of their Tennessee gigs were also cancelled in what lead singer Amy described as a 'policy of hate'.

'Say "cheese", Mr Rose'
On 2 July 1991, the venue for the evening's Guns N' Roses concert was the reassuringly suburban-sounding Riverport Amphitheater in Maryland Heights, Missouri. A fan whipped out his camera and tried to take a photo of lead singer Axl Rose. Shock horror! This unbelievable breach of protocol resulted in Axl yelling at security guards then leaping into the crowd. Within an hour, fifteen police officers and thirty-five members of the audience had been injured. The following night's concert was cancelled because the venue was so badly damaged. A real Kodak moment . . .

Snoop Doggy Duck

Having left the stage of Subterrania in London's Ladbroke Grove after someone (allegedly) tried to shoot him, the Dog returned and offered a £1,000 reward to anyone who could capture his alleged assailant and impress on them that to try and shoot him was not a wise idea. The language he used was slightly more inflammatory than that used above, and included two 'motherfuckers' and two 'fucks' in a twelve-word sentence.

You've got to block, block, block on wood

The Brit Awards again. This time in 2000 – the ceremony in which Robbie Williams challenged Liam Gallagher to a £200,000 televised fist fight after Liam called him a 'fat dancer' and when Ronnie Wood captured the mood of the audience perfectly when he chucked a drink in the face of club DJ Brandon Block as he invaded the stage while Wood and actress Thora Birch were presenting an award. Block and Wood swore at each other as security guards pulled the DJ off the stage.

Very Limp

In 2001, one fan died and sixty were treated for broken limbs and heat exhaustion during Limp Bizkit's appearance at the Sydney Big Day Out festival. The band delayed their set for fifteen minutes but cancelled the rest of the Aussie leg of their tour. The coroner investigating the death blamed lead singer Fred Durst in part for not taking the situation more seriously.

Even Limper

In 2000, at the aptly named Dysfunctional Family Picnic, Fred Durst interrupted his set to verbally assault Creed front-man Scott Stapp, saying, 'He is an egomaniac – he's a fucking punk and right now he's backstage acting like Michael fucking Jackson.'

Or Michael 'fucking allegedly' Jackson, as we must now call him.

Eleven Songs they are A-Changin' (Parts One, Two and Three)

Since 1998, Bob Dylan has toured very consistently with the beginning of the so-called Never-Ending Tour. He starts very promptly at seven-thirty p.m. and never has a support act, so be warned: don't go for a quick pint and turn up at the usual safe time of eight forty-five for the main event, because you will have missed all bar the encores. According to our extensive research there are some 150-plus songs that the Bobster has never ever performed live plus a large number of other ones of which he has performed such obscure versions that no one has recognized them anyway . . .

(PART ONE) THE ELEVEN SONGS PERFORMED MOST FREQUENTLY IN THE FIRST QUARTER OF 2004

'All Along the Watchtower'

'Cat's in the Well'

'Honest with Me'

'Like a Rolling Stone'

'Summer Days'

'Highway 61 Revisited'

'Tweedle Dee & Tweedle Dum'

'Tell Me that it isn't True'

'Stuck Inside of Mobile with the Memphis Blues Again'

'It's Alright, Ma (I'm Only Bleeding)'

'Things Have Changed'

(PART TWO) THE ELEVEN SONGS PERFORMED LEAST FREQUENTLY IN THE FIRST QUARTER OF 2004

'Hazel'

'Desolation Row'

'Dignity'

'Ball and Biscuit'

'God Knows'

'Get Out of Denver'

'Forever Young'

'The Times they are A-Changin' '

'This Wheel's on Fire'

'Silvio'

'To Be Alone with You'

(PART THREE) ELEVEN OF THE MANY SONGS DYLAN HAS NEVER PERFORMED LIVE

'Please Mrs Henry Property of Jesus'

'Sad-Eyed Lady of the Lowlands'

'Sitting on a Barbed Wire Fence'

'I Am a Lonesome Hobo'

'Angel Flying Too Close to the Ground'

'Day of the Locusts'

'Farewell Angelina'

'In Search of Little Sadie'

'Million Dollar Bash'

'Woogie Boogie'

'Nashville Skyline Rag'

Eleven Tour Names: A Quiz

'Tour . . . tour . . . tour,' Nirvana's Dave Grohl once said. 'Ever since I've been in this band, we've been touring. Five nights of playing. Two days of doing press. When we're not on stage, we're eating, or sleeping, or shitting, and that's about it. It's enough to drive anybody insane.'

But surely all this rock-star stress could be relieved if they named their tours something really cool, memorable and different? Every time you see the name stencilled on your luggage, tattooed on your roadies or scrawled on your set list it should give you a lift and a warm feeling inside. Why, then, are so many tour names so boring and so downright macho? Wouldn't it be really refreshing if we had some honesty in this respect? Here's to the S Club Juniors Jailbait tour, the Puberty or Bust(ed) tour and The Rolling Stones' Grumpy Old Men tour.

CAN YOU MATCH THESE TOUR NAMES TO THE RELEVANT BANDS AND YEARS?

1. Drowned World

2. Ticket for Everyone

3. Dangerous World

4. Serious Moonlight

5. Bananas

6. Filthy Lucre

7. World of Our Own

8. A Spanner in the Works

9. Reinvention

10. XS All Areas

11. Rising

Answers

1. Madonna, 2002; 2. Busted, 2003; 3. Michael Jackson, 1991–1992; 4. David Bowie, 1983; 5. Deep Purple, 2004; 6. The Sex Pistols, 1996; 7. Westlife, 2004; 8. Rod Stewart, 1995; 9. Madonna, 2004–2005; 10. Status Quo, 2004–2005; 11. Bruce Springsteen, 2002–2003

BLINDED BY SCIENCE

The Eleven Most Expensive Hi-Fi Components in the World

For most people, choosing new hi-fi equipment is all about asking: 'Can I afford it?' 'Does it look like it's loud?' 'Is it loud?' However, for some there is only one question to answer: 'Is this the best, the very best, that money can buy?'

If you have ever wondered what it might be like to *be* like this, then join us now as we take you on a tour of 'The most high-fidelity hi-fi in the world, ever!'

Sumiko Blue Point Special Stylus ($480)
Why break up a winning team? There's no reason to buy a new stylus when you can ship your original to Australia to be restored by Garrott Brothers Retipping and Stylus Replacement.

Reson Reca Moving Magnet Phono Cartridge ($300)
That little box that the stylus sits in. More important than it looks, so might as well get the best.

Origin Live Illustrious Tonearm ($2,150)
What? You have to buy a separate *arm*? Yes you do, if you really want the best sound. Very few of the top-end decks ship with an arm – they're too busy getting the spinning part just right.

Aurora Gold Turntable ($2,386.75)
At last! Something we understand!

Pass Labs X2.5 Preamplifier ($3,900)
You might ask why you need a *pre*amplifier; if you do ask, you're in the wrong shop, bub.

McIntosh MC1201 Monoblock Power Amplifier ($15,000 per pair)
Big expensive hi-fi amps don't mess about with all that stereo nonsense. They do one thing – and they get it right. Therefore, you'll need at least two matched amps.

Von Gaylord Chinchilla Loudspeaker Cable ($3,600 per 8ft pair)
Special cables now? We wouldn't bother, but we loved their name so much we couldn't resist.

Wilson X1 Grand Slamm Speakers ($75,900 per pair)
These beauties neither look nor sound anything like those little plywood affairs you get from Argos. They're as big as you, and they're more faithful.

Nakamichi CR-7E Cassette Deck (around $950 second-hand)
The serious hi-fi world abandoned the cassette about ten years ago, but you still want to play those mix tapes you've got in that shoebox under the bed, don't you? Nakamichi are the Rolls-Royce of cassette decks.

Gryphon Mikado CD Player ($12,000)
Only distantly related to the average domestic coaster-toaster, this looks wonderful and has a laser that you could use to signal astronauts on Mars, if there were any.

Magnum Dynalab MD-108 Hybrid Analog Reference FM Tuner ($5,850)
Imagine owning a radio so good that, no matter how long you own it, you would genuinely believe that Jonathan Ross was popping round every Saturday. And it's got valves in it! They light up!

Eleven Guitars We Won't Be Getting for Christmas

The purchase of a vintage electric guitar is a luxury known only to rock musicians and a small percentage of financial advisors weathering midlife crises. Most of us can only dream of the following luxuries:

Fender Broadcaster prototype
The progenitor of the most successful electric guitars ever. The Broadcaster, rapidly renamed for copyright reasons the Telecaster, is a squarish plank of wood with a pick-up on it, from which the skilful guitarist can conjure the sound of 'Honky Tonk Woman' or 'Green Onions'. After being exhibited in a Fifty Years of Fender exhibition, this 1949 model sold to an anonymous collector for £200,000.

1927 Martin model 0042
The ultimate acoustic guitar, constructed of Brazilian rosewood in an age when that kind of thing was acceptable. With its original case you could expect to pay in excess of £20,000.

1956 Gibson Switchmaster ES-5
The guitar that says 'jazz'. Perfect for every budding Charlie Christian with £18,500 to spare.

1965 Fender Stratocaster
The classic electric guitar. The instrument of Hank Marvin, Jimi Hendrix and Kurt Cobain. An example with unblemished Candy Apple Red paint would lighten your pocket of £17,000.

1959 Gibson George Gobels L5CT
Scotty Moore, guitarist on all the classic Elvis material, had one of these. His personal instrument would be almost beyond price, but even without star provenance this would set you back around £15–16,000.

1962 Gibson ES355TDC
Back to the Future fans will be familiar with this guitar. Marty plays it at the 1955 high-school dance – regardless of the fact that it wasn't on sale at the time. Oh well, that's time travel for you. Whatever, it's worth £11,000.

1956 Fender Precision Bass
Although electric guitars took some time to evolve from their 1930s beginnings, Leo Fender got the electric bass right first time. We can't tell you how much we want one of these. All we need is £9,000. Each.

1966 Fender Jaguar
Aimed at the jazz instrumentalist but seized upon by the surf scene. A mid-sixties example, especially in a rarer finish like Sea Foam Green, would fetch well over £6,500.

1962 Fender Bass VI
This experiment in extended-range basses never sold particularly well – a fact that only adds to its rarity, and desirability, and price: £6,000 to you.

1958 Gibson Les Paul Junior
This simple, almost primitive instrument is the source of the fat, overdriven sounds of The Sex Pistols and The Clash. Originally introduced as a budget line, today one of these 'cut-price' instruments is yours for around £4,000.

2002 Gibson SG Special 'Pete Townshend'
Although modern, the limited run of only 250 guitars gives it an instant rarity. The guitar has been finished to approximate the exact level of wear on Pete's SG at the time of the 1970 *Live at Leeds* LP. For an extra consideration they'd probably even smash it through a speaker cabinet for you. As it stands, one of these will set you back a little under £3,000.

Eleven Great Producers

No one twiddles knobs quite like the following bunch.

Phil Spector
Phil Spector first saw the power of the studio when he discovered that Duane Eddy's famous guitar twang was helped on its way by messing around with echo and tape speed. From there he developed his 'wall of sound', put to good use on such hits as 'Da Doo Ron Ron' and 'Be My Baby'. Also ruined The Beatles' *Let it Be* and most recently produced Starsailor.

George Martin
The man behind arguably the greatest act of the twentieth century. And as well as producing The Goons he had a hand in some band or other from Liverpool. Avoid at all costs Martin's swansong, *In My Life*, in which various 'friends' such as Jim Carrey and Robin Williams massacre a selection of Beatles classics. Not funny.

Stephen Street
We don't know if there is a street called Stephen Street, but if there is it would be home to a whole host of indie pop stars. Street came to prominence as the producer of The Smiths, and cemented his reputation with his work for Britpop-era Blur.

Trevor Horn
Where to start? The man behind Buggles and 'Video Killed the Radio Star', Trevor Horn went on to produce ABC's *The Lexicon of Love* and 'Relax' by Frankie Goes to Hollywood – respectively *the* classic eighties pop album and single. Like some latterday Brian Wilson, Horn spent a whopping six months getting the Frankie sound right. Other successes include Seal and, er, taTu.

Brian Eno and Daniel Lanois
Brian Eno and Daniel Lanois first pitched up in U2 land for *The*

Unforgettable Fire, with the former Roxy Music synthesist and ambient pioneer mumbling about 'obscure strategies' and the like. U2's music opened up with a new brainy sound big enough to fill stadia. As a rule of thumb, when Eno is on board (*The Joshua Tree, Achtung Baby*) U2 are great and when he's on holiday (*Rattle and Hum*) they're pants.

John Leckie
If Street is the man to ring if you want your band to sound like The Smiths, Leckie is the person to call if you want things a little more sixties-sounding. Leckie's most influential work came with producing XTC's alter egos, The Dukes of Stratosphear. The Stone Roses heard that, and John got the call.

The Neptunes
Creating clipped beats and melodic genius, Pharrell Williams and Chad Hugo have twiddled the knobs for everyone from Britney to Nelly, Justin to Beyoncé and Kelis to Jay-Z. So successful is their touch that in August 2003 their productions accounted for twenty per cent of the songs played on British radio. A sort of twenty-first century Stock, Aitken & Waterman, then, but cooler.

Jam and Lewis
Originally members of The Time, Jimmy Jam and Terry Lewis saw their brand of bump 'n' grind R&B take off with Janet Jackson. They have since gone on to work with, among others, Mariah Carey, Usher, Mary J. Blige, Boyz II Men, Mya . . . and Bryan Adams.

Quincy Jones
In 1969, Buzz Aldrin played Quincy's arrangement of 'Fly Me to the Moon' after he had flown to the moon. In the 1980s, Quincy became a one-word shorthand for slick-production genius: he produced both the bestselling album of all time, Michael Jackson's *Thriller*, and the bestselling US single of all time, 'We Are the World'. Quince-essential.

Mutt Lange
If you want an eighties rock sound wide enough to fill an ice-hockey stadium, Mutt is your man. Making his name producing AC/DC's *Highway to Hell* and *Back in Black*, Mutt (real name Robert) went on to turn the knobs up to eleven for Foreigner, Def Leppard, The Cars and Huey Lewis. In the nineties he married Shania Twain. Now her drums are big, too.

Butch Vig
Nirvana, The Smashing Pumpkins, Sonic Youth, L7: Butch was the bloke behind them all. *Nevermind*, of course, is his act in a nutshell – his simple, crunching sound managed to be both alternative and mainstream, providing

the grunge blueprint that many would imitate but never better. After that, it was all Garbage.

Eleven Albums with a Tortuous Recording History

Sometimes, albums are recorded in a matter of weeks with the minimum of fuss. The trouble is, they're shit. Any decent record has a back story of tantrums, arguments, budgets spiralling out of control and deadlines being missed by years. In fact, some of the following took so long to finish, they might even have set records.

The Second Coming by The Stone Roses
Like any proper collection of red-blooded males, The Roses couldn't come again as quickly as they'd like. The first album came out in 1989. This follow-up appeared five years later. Legal disputes and changes of record label didn't help, but did it actually take them years to record the album? Did it heck. After much faffing about, they knocked it out in a year.

The Seeds of Love by Tears for Fears
Unlike this pair, who spent four years arguing and re-recording before releasing this, their third album. Seeing Oleta Adams in a hotel bar was a turning point. They wasted ages trying to recreate her sound before going back to the hotel and getting her on the album.

...Yes Please by The Happy Mondays
The band went to the Bahamas in the hope of keeping Shaun away from the drugs. It didn't work. Producers Chris Frantz and Tina Weymouth pulled their hair out. Factory Records got a bill for a quarter of a million pounds and went bust.

Loveless by My Bloody Valentine
If Factory's money went on The Mondays, then Creation's went the Valentines' way, to the tune of £200,000. Technologically speaking, everything that could go wrong did go wrong. Trying to set up a tent in which to record the guitar didn't help. Bloody great, though.

The one after Loveless by My Bloody Valentine
Still incomplete, the band's 'first' record for Island records has yet to

materialize. With four songs complete in more than as many years, the band offered to put them out as an EP. The record company optimistically decided to 'save' them for the album. They are still waiting.

The Menace by Elastica
If you are a prog band, then there at least is some justification for spending five years recording your second album. If, however, your *raison d'être* is short, sharp, pop punk, there is simply no excuse.

Deep Down and Dirty by The Stereo MCs
Elastica seem like speedy workers compared to this lot and the nine years it took them to follow up *Connected*.

Smile by The Beach Boys
Good Vibrations took six months to record. Then the vibrations got very bad indeed.

Dog Man Star by Suede
Bernard's dad died. Brett hired a haunted house for inspiration. The nineties' Morrissey and Marr split up.

Kid A by Radiohead
Thom Yorke was up to here with guitars. This was not good news if you were a guitar player in a guitar band. Sessions have been happier.

Searching for the Young Soul Rebels by Dexy's Midnight Runners
Kevin wasn't happy with the record company. Kevin procured the master tapes. Kevin refused to give them back until the contract was rewritten. Guess what? It worked.

Eleven Great Hidden Tracks and Messages

Bang! by World Party
Patchy follow-up to *Goodbye Jumbo* saves the best until last. Hold your finger down on the final track until it hits eighteen minutes and out comes a glorious Beach Boys pastiche, updating 'Surfing USA' to 1991 and setting it in Kuwait City. Gulf War jokes aplenty.

The Second Coming by The Stone Roses
The track-counter says ninety-nine, but beyond track twelve, 'Love Spreads', there is silence until track ninety. The band plink about out of tune on a piano. Didn't make it on to their greatest hits.

Think Tank by Blur
An ingenious third way of concealing that extra track: this time it's hidden before the start of the album. Press play, press pause, press rewind. At minus-five minutes or so, Blur and Phil Daniels are reunited all over again.

Kid A by Radiohead
Copies from the first run of the album contain a hidden booklet. Clue: you have to take the CD case apart to find it.

Sgt. Pepper's Lonely Hearts Club Band by The Beatles
High-pitched noises that only your dog could hear.

The Wall by Pink Floyd
'.Chatford ,farm funny the of care ,Pink Old to answer your send Please .message secret the discovered just You've' message the contains 'Spaces Empty' track the ,backwards Played.

'Another One Bites the Dust' by Queen
A backwards message that doesn't really exist. It's claimed that you'll hear 'Let's smoke marijuana'. You won't. You'll hear 'Lessip mok marid udjuina'.

In Utero by Nirvana
Twenty minutes after 'All Apologies' finishes, up pops 'Gallons of Rubbing Alcohol Flow Through the Strip'.

How to Cut and Paste the Eighties by DJ Yoda
How do you end an eighties cut-and-paste album for people who haven't switched off? Why, with Ferris Bueller's post-credits comments, of course.

'Fire on High' by ELO
The backwards message says: 'The music is reversible but time is not . . . turn back! Turn back! Turn back!'

This Year's Model by Elvis Costello
Scratched into the run-off groove of initial pressings was the message 'Special Pressing No. 003. Ring Moira on 434 3232 for your special prize'. Moira got a lot of phone calls.

Eleven Records Made by DJs

A random selection of eleven absolutely cracking records made by people who should – by rights – just be playing them.

'The Adventures of Grandmaster Flash on the Wheels of Steel' by Grandmaster Flash and the Furious Five
The daddy of them all. The closest anyone has ever come to capturing the art of a great DJ on vinyl.

'Convoy UK' by Laurie Lingo and the Dipsticks
The Hairy Cornflake. The closest anyone has come to capturing a hirsute breakfast cereal on vinyl.

'The Floral Dance' by Terry Wogan
One hundred per cent baffling. Will anyone who bought this single please send us a letter (we can't believe you're allowed email where you are) explaining why.

'Planet Rock' by Afrika Bambaata and the Soul Sonic Force
Classic robot funk. Easy listening for Transformers.

'Let's All Chant' by Pat Sharpe and Mick Brown
The singing haircut and Europe's premier Hawaiian-shirt connoisseur together on record for the first (and last, we hope) time!

'Let Me Clear My Throat' by DJ Kool
This really is good. If you only check out one record by a DJ after reading this book, make it this one.

'Bow Down Krishna' by Boy George
Former new-romantic legend buys some decks, stops washing his neck properly and sings a song about Harry Ramsden or something. Within months, cod is extinct in northern-European waters.

'Wash Your Face in My Sink' by The Dream Warriors
Canadian DJ/rap combo offers advice to Boy George. Within months, nothing happens.

'On the Beat' by George Formby featuring DJ Yoda
2Many DJs' more playful cousin gets busy with The Lancashire Lad.

As Heard on Radio Soulwax, Volumes 1 to 12 by 2Many DJs
The masters of mash-up make twelve albums. Only release one (Volume 2). Dang lawyers!

'It Feels So Good' by Sonique
Proper singer turns DJ, then makes record with proper singing on it. Hit ensues. Clever.

Eleven Bits of Technology that Changed Rock 'n' Roll

Technology is the stuff that makes rock 'n' roll happen. Even an acoustic guitar is, in its little wooden heart, technology.

Les Paul
Well, Les might not count as technology, but his stupendously heavy guitars do – and they alone are enough to make him a legend. In fact his legacy is greater even than that: he more or less invented the multi-tracking and over-dubbing techniques that led to the densely orchestrated progressive-rock recordings of bands like Yes and Talk Talk. Yeah, thanks a lot, Les.

The synthesizer
The story of the synthesizer really starts in the third century BC, when a Greek engineer named Ktesibios built a sort of organ that worked using air- and water-pressure and was called a Hyraulos. If we linger there, though, it'll take a long time to get anywhere interesting, so let's skip forward to Bob Moog. Although Bob didn't make the first synthesizers, he made the first usable, popular ones. One of the earliest all-Moog recordings was Walter (later to become Wendy) Carlos's *Switched-On Bach*.

The Mellotron
The Mellotron was the first instrument to capture and reproduce the sounds of other instruments. Essentially a bank of tape machines, it took the majesty of a symphony orchestra or the sheer bombast of a jazz big band and turned them, and indeed any other sound you could imagine, into that wheezy-woozy wave that always says The Moody Blues. You can buy samples of the Mellotron to load into the latest samplers, which suggests that the appeal of the drunken violinists will never die.

The Marshall Stack
Jim Marshall built his first amplifiers in 1962 at the behest of pop musicians who were unable to hear their little WEM and Vox amps over the gale of screams that emanated from the seat-wetting Beatlemaniacs. Driving the new amps to their limit led to a new sound, valve distortion, that ultimately gave birth to heavy metal. Cheers, Jim.

The drum machine
No single innovation divided the creative minds of rock as dramatically as did Roger Linn's 'drum machine', the Linn Drum. Months after it first appeared in 1979, the UK Top Ten was composed almost entirely of music *underpinned* by the characteristic snare sound of the Linn Mark I. The inimitable flabby thud, reminiscent of damp cardboard being struck with mange-tout, made hundreds of session drummers redundant at a stroke and led directly to a marked increase in the quantity of interior decorators in the Greater London area.

The fuzzbox
The fuzzbox was one of many sound-boosting devices created by naval acoustics experts Roger Mayer, and it made the guitar sound very much like a comb and paper being played by an adenoidal wasp. Big Jim Sullivan was the first to actually commit this evil sound to vinyl, with his solo on P.J. Proby's 'Hold Me'. From that day forth, guitarists strove to mangle the fundamentally pleasing tone of their instruments in ever more unlikely ways.

AutoTune – the secret weapon of the karaoke revolution
Before AutoTune, the pop-music gene pool was confined to the comparatively narrow confluence of two streams of humanity: those who could sing, and those who were easy on the eye. Dr Harold Hildebrand's invention obviated the necessity for the search for some mythical *chimera* with the pulchritude of a Fabian and the vocal power of a Rik Waller, and gave rise to the boy-band explosion that we still enjoy to this day. Tremendous.

The Fender Precision Bass
Clarence Leonidas Fender was born to a family of Californian orange farmers in 1909. He lost his job during the Depression and decided to turn his hobby, repairing radios, into a full-time business. This led, for reasons we will never understand, to a lucrative sideline in electric-guitar design. In 1950, he launched the Fender Precision Bass. If you have ever heard a pop-music record, you have heard a Fender bass – or a bass that wishes it were a Fender.

Roland – the future is now

Possibly more than any other products, Roland synthesizers and drum machines define the sound of modern dance music. Roland's TR808, with its characteristic 'Sexual Healing' percussion and sonic-boom bass drum, still underpins most hip-hop recordings twenty years after the original machine was discontinued. The 808 was followed by the 909, which became the drum box of choice for the Chicago house scene; the TB303 became the sound of acid house. Roland were not tempted to round out the range with a drum machine designated '404'. The number four sounds a little bit like 'death' in several Oriental languages and is thus considered unlucky.

The Gizmotron

It made your guitar sound a bit like some violins. A certain suspension of disbelief was required, though: really it sounded quite a bit more like some little plastic wheels rubbing on the strings.

The Atari ST

It's hard to imagine the acid-house scene without the little plastic heart of the Atari ST – though for those of us who were involved in the scene it's hard to imagine anything at all these days. It was widely reported at the time that the 'ST' in the Atari's name stood for 'Sam Tramiel'. Of course, it didn't – it stood for 'sixteen thirty-two'. It's something to do with the inside of the computer, apparently. We don't care about that. We just keep having flashbacks to a muddy field and flashing lights.

Eleven Bits of Music We Could Live Without

Music files on computers can be big. It's more convenient if they're little. They download faster from Napster and you can store more on your hard disk/MP3 player/keyring/toaster. A clever man called Frauenhofer invented an encoding and decoding system (a 'codec', for you *Star Trek* fans out there) that works out which bits of the music you can't hear and doesn't bother including them. We got to thinking how much better it would be if it went one further . . . Every great song contains a boring bit that the band couldn't get right; every classic album – especially now, in the era of the so-called bonus track – has the one that Ringo sings. Here are eleven things that should disappear when we convert the CD to the MP3.

The intro from 'Don't You Forget About Me'

If there's one single that could be found to represent the eighties, this is it: the song that everyone remembers from *The Breakfast Club*. It's a cracker, as long as you can survive the painful first four bars. The introductory spontaneous emoting on the record somehow evokes dads dancing at weddings, coppers skanking at the Notting Hill Carnival and giraffes bending down to drink. The miracle is that it summons up all these images at once. No one can listen to that depressing display of artificial exuberance and not feel at least a momentary twinge of pity for poor Jim.

'Rat-ta-tat-ta-tat' from 'Chanson D'Amour'

Nothing more to say here. It was a mistake. It should never have happened. Manhattan Transfer. It was them. Move along, nothing to see . . .

Pretty much all of 'D'Yer Mak'er'

The Zeppelin followed their all-conquering 'No title as such, but there's a chap on the front with some sticks' album with *Houses of the Holy*, almost entirely a classic record. Ostensibly an attempt to exploit the growing cachet of reggae, 'D'Yer Mak'er' rapidly devolves into a lumpy doo-wop pastiche punctuated by Bonzo's wildly inappropriate drum fills. It's a horrible song. Herr Frauenhofer, the screens . . .

The bit with the cheap-synthesizer pan-pipes from 'Laura'

The Scissor Sisters' first album is a non stop cavalcade of good old-fashioned songwriting, reminiscent of those wonderful days when Sir Elton John didn't wear suits made out of curry-house wallpaper. They clearly didn't want to make it *too* accessible, however – the album opens with the most annoying sixteen bars of music ever. It sounds like a frightening fairground ride.

The Soup Dragon attack from 'Party in Session'

Black Uhuru were the reggae band that even people who hated reggae grudgingly admired. Theirs was a package so complete that you might consider any additional personnel unnecessary – certainly if they turned out to be The Clangers. Nevertheless a group of space mice are very much in evidence on the instrumental section of Uhuru's 1984 classic 'Party in Session', whistling and tweeting for all they are worth. You'd be forgiven for thinking that some kind of prescribed herbal medication had been administered to Puma, Duckie & Co.

Tom dancing during 'Kiss'

We're not talking about the Prince version here. No, we're addressing the cover version which more-or-less reinvented leather-trousered, leather-skinned, leather-lunged bingo totty Tom Jones. Producers The Art of Noise were somewhat stumped by the guitar-solo section; lacking a guitarist, they pasted together random sequences from their back catalogue. At a listen, however, what makes the experience truly unbearable is Tom's announcement that he's about to dance through this bit. We've got an idea what Tom dancing looks like and it isn't pretty. A little tactful masking required.

Bryan whistling on 'Jealous Guy'
Released so soon after John Lennon's untimely death that one is tempted to think that someone in Roxy Music's organization had access to Mark Chapman's diary, 'Jealous Guy' is by no means the most impressive entry in the Roxy canon. Nevertheless, circumstances conspired to make it number one in the days when that still meant something. No amount of sentiment, though, will make that whistling bit acceptable.

Madonna's shopping list in 'American Life'
Madonna is a truly great pop star, but – oh dear, oh dear, oh *dear* – she's an atrocious rapper. We must take issue with her ill-advised essay at getting 'ill' in the middle-eight section of her single 'American Life'. The simple fact is that she sounds like Rex Harrison.

Rolf breaking the rules in 'Two Little Boys'
A simple one, this: you can't rhyme a word with itself. You could be drummed out of the Musicians' Union for that kind of thing. It's common sense, then, that rhyming a word with itself in *the chorus of the song*, so it comes up seven or eight times in the record, is the purest evil. Rolf, of all people. How does he sleep?

Bob's muse deserts him – 'Wiggle Wiggle'
People of a certain generation will try to tell you what a wonderful poet Bob Dylan is. Play them this.

What is he *saying* in 'Blinded by the Light'?
Bruce Springsteen's another one known for his lyrical prowess. Not on this track he isn't. Please email us if you know a) what he's saying or b) what it *means*.

Eleven Questions You Never Knew You Wanted to Ask about CDs

For most young Britons, the first intimation that a new music-carrier was on the horizon was one of those quixotically optimistic announcements on *Tomorrow's World*. The first real-world application was, perhaps disappointingly, Billy Joel's *52nd Street*. Creatively tapped out by the grind of promoting his previous album, the spaniel-eyed downtown guy had produced a stop-gap album to sate his legions of fans, accountants and A&R men. Perhaps in its prescient anticipation of the next quarter century of music, it should now be hailed as the all-time classic that Billy so obviously wanted it to be.

How long does a CD last?
Official figures in the original CD spec suggest a lifetime of anything between seventy and two hundred years. Real-world tests suggest that a CD of great funk tracks burnt in a Macintosh computer then left in a Volkswagen will begin to noticeably degrade after two years.

When was the CD actually invented?
The initial idea for a small disc encoded with digital music dates back to 1972, but there were a number of changes along the way, including an extra 5mm added to the diameter in 1979.

Why is a CD seventy-four minutes long?
There is an urban legend that the playing time of a CD was based on the length of Beethoven's Symphony No. 9. German conductor Herbert von Karajan, a top Sony executive and the wife of a top Sony executive are all suspected of having suggested this particular running time. Bearing in mind the availability nowadays of CDs with play times in excess of eighty minutes, the original specification does appear to have been pretty arbitrary.

So, I hear that the sample rate of a CD is 44.1 kHz. What's all that about, then?
Officially, the average human ear can perceive frequencies up to about 20 kHz. Some science guy called Nyquist explained why you have to sample at twice that rate. The original digital audio recorders were repurposed professional video recorders and it just so happens that 44.1 kHz is within the range of both English and American machines.

There's a laser in there? Cool! Can I shoot anyone with it? Can I use it to write my name on a CD?
Yes, no, and not really. Yamaha came up with their 'disc tattoo' system back in 2002, claiming that it could etch designs on to the CD using the laser. If you're the kind of person who understands those annoying 'magic eye' pictures, you might be able to make out the designs. *Might*.

Hooray! Digital always beats analogue!
Not quite true. Generally speaking, cheap digital sounds better than cheap analogue, but most Hollywood movies and proper records are still mastered on analogue gear. They aren't doing it that way for fun.

CDs are easier to make than vinyl – is piracy a problem?
It's estimated that around a third of CDs on sale are pirate copies.

So when did the bootleggers catch up?
In 1987, when a CD containing much of the material from The Beatles' 1995 *Anthology* and 2003 *Let It Be, Naked* began to appear on market stalls.

How many CDs are there in the world?
About 2.4 billion pre-recorded CDs are sold annually. The number of blank CDs sold is about the same as that.

I'm bored now; tell me something interesting!
Jeanne Louise Calment released a CD on her 121st birthday, in 1996. Called *Time's Mistress*, it features her reminiscing over a hip-hop background.

I've heard loads of things about improving the sound of CDs by freezing them/drawing on them, etc. Is there any truth in any of that?
No.

Eleven Records that Escaped from the Studio

Cast your mind back to a more innocent age, when 'bootlegs' were simply recordings for which there was a demand but no legitimate means of release. Since sound recordings did not receive proper copyright protection in the USA until 15 February 1972, discs like Dylan's *Great White Wonder* received wider distribution than the bootlegs of today. Here are eleven of the most interesting.

Bright Lights, Big City by The Rolling Stones

A collection of unreleased studio recordings from '63 and '64, featuring such enduring classics as 'Diddley Daddy' and 'Crackin' Baby'. More sensitive readers can console themselves that at least 'Cocksucker Blues' isn't on it.

Get Back by The Beatles

Since released as *Let It Be, Naked*, *Get Back* is George Martin's take on The Beatles' penultimate studio recording and final release. Stripped of Phil Spector's orchestral 'sweetening', the material gives a far clearer sense of the band's state of mind at the time. We would direct your attention to the woefully listless bass-guitar effort on 'The Long and Winding Road'. Maybe The Beatles released the right record first time round?

The Great White Wonder by Bob Dylan

In 1967, soon after his fabled motorcycle accident, Bob Dylan holed up with a backing band – inventively called The Band – in Saugerties, NY. They recorded around 100 songs, including covers of tracks by Curtis Mayfield and Johnny Cash. The results of these sessions weren't released at the time, but acetates found their way into the hands of celebrity Dylan fans like Peter, Paul & Mary, The Byrds and even Manfred Mann – all of whom immediately released covers of the new Dylan material. A selection of the original demos was eventually given an official release (as *The Basement Tapes*) in 1975, by which time anyone who cared already had the widely distributed bootleg or had forgotten the 1960s altogether.

Who's Zoo by The Who

A compilation of hard-to-find official recordings and TV spots collated with love by diehard American Who fans and wrapped in one of the strangest record sleeves imaginable: depicting the band as a lion, a camel, a gnu and a gorilla respectively (we think you can guess which is who), it anticipates Jeanine Pettibone's pioneering stage-costume designs for Spiñal Tap by some years.

Session Man by James Patrick Page

This is strictly one for Zep completists. As the title suggests, this is a collection of Jimmy's session work before he joined The Yardbirds. It includes the indispensable 'Leave My Kitten Alone' by The First Gear and of course Bobby Graham's 'Zoom, Widge, and Wag'.

The Black Album by Prince

In 1985, Prince was at the top of his game. He recorded the brilliant if underrated *Parade* album and released his second movie, the frankly rather silly *Under the Cherry Moon*. Then something snapped and Prince became a bootlegger's dream. He recorded and then abandoned an album with The Revolution, called *Dream Factory*, then recorded another album, on his own, known as *The Black Album* – a collection of rude, crude and loopy funk tracks. While waiting for *that* to be released, Prince recorded a triple-album's worth of material which he planned to call *The Crystal Ball*, but he abandoned that, too, and instead released the comparatively straightforward *Lovesexy*. Many of the *Crystal Ball* songs found their way on to *Sign o' the Times*, but *The Black Album* was held in limbo until 1994, by which time anyone who cared . . .

Psychedelic Games for May by Pink Floyd
A compilation of early studio recordings, *PGFM* captures the paisley-scarfed Syd Barrett-era Floyd, when Jenny Fabian still travelled in their van and Roger Waters wore novelty sunglasses. It features versions of songs from their first album proper, *Piper at the Gates of Dawn*, together with relics of their blues-band past and portents of Syd's wigged-out future.

The Troggs Tapes by The Troggs
Not exactly an album, but we couldn't resist. The sessions for their projected *Tranquillity* album were anything but tranquil. The recording of the band exhorting each other to make the record a 'number fucken one' became an instant classic. The ten-minute tape is full of one-liners that are now part of studio parlance the world over: 'Sprinkle a bit of fucken fairy dust on it'; 'You big pranny.'

21 Tracks by Radiohead
Twenty-one otherwise unreleased tracks from rock's glummest superband, all on a cheery picture CD showing some chubby lad with a load of make-up on. Of course, the politically aware rockers would prefer you to buy this CD from Yellow Fish Records rather than anything from that nasty multinational EMI. Oh. No, they wouldn't.

Big Fat 45 by KLF
Perhaps one of the weirdest of all. An authentically packaged but horrible-sounding EP of mash-ups which purports to be made by the originators of the genre but is more likely to have been made by a couple of members of The Pooh Sticks.

Vertigo by U2
We'd love to have had a Webcam in the room when Bono found out that a CD-Rom of this album had been lost somewhere in France. 'You lost *what*? This isn't the first time, Edge, you eejit; there was the 1991 studio sessions as well – can't you get a bag, like a normal fella, instead of keeping all your CDs in your hat?'

Eleven Songs about Technology

Modern musicians have an intimate relationship with the technology of sound. Sometimes, sitting in a studio full of instruments and amplifiers, they're tempted to write about their surroundings. Especially when they can't think of anything else to write about. Here are eleven of our favourite songs about the machines they use to make the songs.

'Electric Guitar' by Talking Heads (electric guitars)
Long before broadsheet respectability and roomy tailoring, Talking Heads were an artier-than-most New York new-wave band looking for a way to stand out from the crowd of their thinner, paler, loopier contemporaries. The Eno-produced angular funk of their *Fear of Music* LP was the unique selling-point they needed. Languishing towards the end of this album is 'Electric Guitar'. It's a mildly disturbing tale of electric guitars being run over and then, inexplicably, put on trial. Upsetting.

'Synthesizer' by Electric Six (the synthesizer)
In 2003, Electric Six burst on to a pop-music scene starved of Ronald Coleman moustaches and gay Abraham Lincolns with their wilfully silly album *Fire*. Languishing towards the end of this album (do we see a pattern here?) is a paean to that most modern and exciting of instruments, the synthesizer. Dickie Valentine makes it abundantly clear that no amount of coughing in anyone's face will halt the irrepressible force of his techno.

'6 Reasons' by D12 (the many uses for keyboard instruments)
Of course, the synthesizer is but one of the many keyboard instruments available to the creative musician. One thinks instantly of the Clavioline, without which the Tornadoes' memorable hit 'Telstar' would have been a rather dull rhythm track. The most wonderful thing about keyboard instruments is their weight and sheer stopping power in a brawl situation. We would like to quote D12, who speak of 'Busting DJs over their backs with keyboards'. Now, you wouldn't want to get in a scrap with someone holding a Hammond organ if all you had was a harmonica, would you?

'Dance On' by Prince (the bass guitar)
We think Prince puts it best when at the beginning of 'Dance On' from his *Lovesexy* album, he tells us that 'There's a bass guitar in this.'
   He's right. There is.

'Was it all Worth It?' by Queen (drums)
In this song from Queen's *The Miracle* album, Roger Taylor describes

buying a drum kit and goes on to ask, 'Was it all worth it?' Well, of course it was, Roger. You're a millionaire.

'The Beautiful Ones' by Suede (the drum machine)

The drum machine has become a much-loved member of many modern acts. Echo & the Bunnymen named their group after theirs. You can hear it on 'In the Air Tonight' and you can hear it on 'Planet Rock'. It's a reliable little pal that never turns up late for rehearsals and never brings its girlfriend.

'We are the Robots' by Kraftwerk (robots)

Even a cursory glance at the members of Kraftwerk leads one to suspect that they may, indeed, be the robots. Robots *always* wear red shirts and lipstick – it's in Isaac Asimov's rules or something. The teutonic techno-tinklers even deployed a quartet of lookalike robots on tour, to see if anyone noticed. No one did. They were too impressed by the sound of Florian's pocket calculator.

'Wired for Sound' by Sir Cliff Richard (the Walkman)

Whether AM or FM, he felt so fantastic – and, of course, so he should. In the early days of the Walkman it seemed an impossible dream to hear such fidelity from a cassette in a box. Getting the radio on it as well must have been an *incredible* bonus. Heaven 17 were similarly impressed, and produced *Music for Stowaways* exclusively for Mr Ibuka's little toy.

'C30 C60 C90 Go!' by Bow Wow Wow (the audio cassette)

It's difficult to imagine the record industry getting itself all hot and bothered about a new piece of technology that was set to make it easier to copy music and would probably end in the collapse of the music business, Western civilization, and – ooh, *we* don't know – a big meringue. The *bête noire* of the day was the humble cassette, and the reaction was the somewhat hysterical Home Taping is Killing Music campaign. Cue chaos specialist Malcolm McLaren, a bunch of young men wearing pirate costumes, and a young lady wearing as little as she could get away with. It wasn't a bad record. One of us used to have it. On cassette. But another one of us has just paid £0.79 to download it *legally*.

'She Blinded Me with Science' by Thomas Dolby (science in general)

We're not convinced that Thomas was blinded by anyone at all. We think he just wore those specs to look clever and scientific. Loopy wild-haired boffin Magnus Pyke contributed to Thomas's single, mainly by shouting 'science' whenever he heard a gap. We're assuming that the stately Sir Patrick Moore was busy that day.

'Pacific 202', 'Pacific 303', '606', 'Pacific 809:98', 'Pacific 808080808'
and 'Pacific 909' by 808 State (Roland synthesizers)
808 State's entire output is a tribute to the wonders of the Roland
synthesizer company. Even their name references the electronic drum box,
prized for its bowel-loosening kick drum – the drum machine most
frequently used in dance music. The thing we think all these dance-music
chaps overlook is this: you don't always *want* your bowels loosened. It
may not be very rock 'n' roll of us, but as we end this chapter we'd like to
leave you with this thought: look after your bowels, and they will look
after you.

LET'S TALK ABOUT SEX

Eleven Stars Talking Dirty

Jessica Simpson
'I promised God, my father and my future husband that I would remain a virgin until I got married. I just always knew it was something I wanted to do.'

Michael Jackson
'Why can't you share your bed? The most loving thing to do is to share your bed with someone. It's very charming. It's very sweet. It's what the whole world should do.'

Britney Spears
'My views on virginity have not changed. I want to wait to have sex until I'm married. I do. I want to wait, but it's hard. I just want to live my life.'

Axl Rose
'I'm pro-heterosexual. I can't get enough of women. I have sex as often as possible . . . It's not easy to be in a one-on-one relationship if the other person is not going to allow me to be with other people.'

Boy George
'I like to say that I'm bisexual . . . When I want sex, I buy it.'

Elton John
'I think people should be free to engage in any sexual practices they choose; they should draw the line at goats, though.'

Eminem
'Don't do drugs, don't have unprotected sex, don't be violent . . . Leave that to me.'

Madonna
'Everyone probably thinks that I'm a raving nymphomaniac, that I have an insatiable sexual appetite, when the truth is I'd rather read a book.'

Billy Joel
'There's nothing better than good sex. But bad sex? A peanut butter and jelly sandwich is better than bad sex.'

Sting
'I think I mentioned to Bob [Geldof] I could make love for eight hours. What I didn't say was that this included four hours of begging and then dinner and a movie.'

The Osbournes
Ozzy: 'Jack's up in his room planning his future.'
Sharon: 'The only thing he's planning is his next wank; whether he's going to use his left hand or his right hand.'

Eleven Rock Stars and How they Measure Up (Part Two)

In 1968 Miss Cynthia Plaster Caster of Chicago began making plaster casts of rock stars' penises in varying degrees of – how shall we put this? – 'happiness', and the occasional pair of breasts. Here, in Cynthia's own words, are her descriptions of the Top Eleven plaster casts.

Wayne Kramer (guitarist, MC5)
A vein snakes downward only to get prematurely cropped, along with the rest of the kaboodle. Although ball-less, it's spunky and determined. Length: 1¾ in.

Momus (singer/songwriter)
A flaccid rendering of the alleged 'second-largest in Britain'-ness. It peeks out of an uncircumcised, delicately veined shaft, hunched over the testicles. The tip is a little flattened, probably from a water bubble in the mould. Length: 2 in.

Noel Redding (bassist, The Jimi Hendrix Experience)
The first 'twistie' of several in my collection, which resembles a 'worm peeking out of the ground'. Length: 3⅝ in.

Ronnie Barnett (bassist, The Muffs)
A rugged texture complements this graceful pirouette. His dick was a figure skater with a pointed head and a muscular body. He softened as the

mould went hard, although my souvenir Washington Monument and Empire State Building had been removed from sight and mind by request. Length: 3⁷/₈ in.

Anthony Newley (singer/songwriter)
Average length and circumference, bent just above the testicles. Of Cockney descent – or rather, ascent. Length: 4¾ in.

Clint 'Poppie' Mansell (singer, Pop Will Eat Itself)
A question-mark, throbbing with veins and leftover wrinkled skin . . . brings to mind Rodin's statue *The Thinker*. Length: 4¾ in.

Danny Doll Rodd (singer, The Doll Rodds)
Under an oversized head, a slim, veiny shaft sits in a pair of plump, juicy testicles like a candle on a cupcake. The head then turns to say hello. Length: 4⁵/₈ in.

Zal Yanovsky (lead guitarist, The Lovin' Spoonful)
Compact head, innocuous shaft buttressed to one testicle by a seminiferous tubule. Length: 5 in.

Jimi Hendrix (god)
The Penis de Milo. His long, thick shaft combined with his disproportionately small head brings a shudder to the spinal cord! His pubes got stuck in the mould and at his show that evening he was seen scratching his crotch a lot on stage. Length: 5⁷/₈ in.

Mary Baker (singer, Gaye Bykers on Acid)
A plaster caster's wet dream. Crisp detailing of a lovely stiffie with great composition. The shaft is sizable with a slightly flattened head and squished testicles. Length: 6¹/₈ in.

Margaret Doll Rodd (singer/guitarist, The Doll Rodds)
Two bouncing, sweet baby mega-hunks of plaster. Note: tit casts come with hooks conveniently attached for easy wall mounting and dumbstruck gazing. If you'd rather display them in a prone position, nipples skyward, please request NO HOOKS.

You can see these in throbbing 3 D and buy replicas online or make a welcome contribution to the Cynthia P. Caster Foundation, which offers financial assistance to musicians and artists, at www.cynthiapcaster.org

Eleven Rock-Star Urban Sex Myths . . . Maybe

In one sense whether or not they're true doesn't really matter – they are still great fun to spread around . . .

A Mars a day helps you work, rest and play
Rumour has it that, during a 1967 raid, police discovered Mick Jagger and Marianne Faithfull enjoying a Mars bar. We are not going to draw you a diagram here but, needless to say, the rug would definitely have needed a dry-clean afterwards. There is no evidence at all to support this story. Verdict: calorific nonsense.

Fish supper
In 1969, members of Led Zeppelin reportedly tied a willing red-haired groupie to a bed in a Washington hotel and then did stuff to her with an unspecified number of small mud-sharks. No concrete evidence exists, but later rumours allege that the fish was dead and it was a red snapper, not a shark. That's OK, then. Verdict: great story but smells a bit fishy to us.

10cc and a little bit more
'A friend of my mother works in the local hospital here and last Tuesday at midnight [*insert name of any star*] came in complaining of severe nausea and cramps. When [*his/her*] stomach was pumped and the contents analysed, they were found to contain a gallon of fresh semen. Everyone present was sworn to secrecy.' Verdict: leaves a nasty taste in the mouth.

Bachelor boy
For years, Sir Cliff Richard has been dogged by rumours that he has a secret boyfriend, though there's never been any supporting evidence whatsoever, of course. Sir Cliff has said that he is 'aware of the rumours but I am not gay', and that he lost his virginity to a young lady in the 1960s, but has been celibate ever since. Verdict: Sir Cliff himself has also pointed out that Saint Paul never got married either . . . So Cliff's story must be the Gospel truth, then.

Stolen kisses
Pamela Anderson and Mötley Crüe star Tommy Lee's 1995 personal hardcore video was 'stolen' from their home by a 'builder' and turned up on the Internet. No 'builder' has ever been traced or prosecuted and after many court actions Tommy and Pamela have 'reluctantly' entered into a financial agreement permitting showings on the Net. Verdict: doesn't really seem like 'theft', does it?

Under cover of the knight

In 1990, Angie Bowie said she had once walked in on David Bowie and Mick Jagger in bed together. A week later the guys had issued formal denials and Angie was saying, 'I certainly didn't catch anyone in the act . . . They happened to be naked and they happened to be David Bowie and Mick Jagger – it doesn't necessarily mean it was some sort of affair.' Verdict: oh, Angieeee.

Like a virgin

Rumour has occasionally linked Madonna with other women – Courtney Love and Kelly McGillis among them. Madge has said: 'Whether I slept with Sandra Bernhard or not is irrelevant. I'm perfectly willing to have people think that I did. You know, I'd almost rather they thought that I did. Just so they could know that here is this girl that everyone was buying records of, and she was eating someone's pussy.' Whether or not this is a theme destined to end up in her next children's book has yet to be announced. Verdict: whatever.

Does he beat it?

Michael Jackson insists that he is the natural father of his two kids but sources close to Debbie Rowe have alleged that she was artificially inseminated with anonymously donated sperm. Verdict: whether the children are ebony or ivory, we doubt that the family will be living together in perfect harmony.

taTu you

In 2003, teenage 'schoolgirl lovers' Lena Katina and Julia Volkova burst on to the scene with their massive hit 'All the Things She Said'. The paedo-pop video was widely banned but this lesbian thing never really rang true and the fact that their manager subsequently described them as an 'underage sex project' didn't really help to maintain the façade. Oh yes, and then Julia Volkova got pregnant . . . Verdict: lipstick heterosexuals.

Scream if you wanna go faster

Did Ginger Geri and Robbie Williams enjoy a Summer of Love? On BBC Radio One, Robbie gallantly said that 'We are just good friends who have the occasional shag' and that 'I was in the Spice Girls – well at least two of them', but Geri insisted that she saw him as her long-lost twin brother and that sex was not on the menu. Verdict: well-timed hype to sell records.

Cock DJ

Is Robbie (him again) bisexual, and did he enjoy a secret relationship with his one-time housemate Jonathan Wilkes? Robbie once said, 'If I meet a man I fancy enough to have sex with, I will.' But Wilkes is certainly off the menu, as the Rev. Robbie Williams recently 'married' him and his wife in a civil ceremony. Verdict: keep 'em guessing, Robbie!

'Fancy a Night-Cap?': Eleven Songs to Play Your Lover (Parts One and Two)

(PART ONE) GET IT ON

As part of our public service here is a soundtrack that will guarantee that the atmosphere stays seductive and loving. (Incidentally, it lasts only thirty-nine minutes so do get on with it.)

'Mystic Lady' by T.Rex

'Let's Get it On' by Marvin Gaye

'Protection' by Massive Attack

'Hot in Herre' by Nelly and Dani Stevenson

'Turn Me On' by Norah Jones

'Hot Love Now' by The Wonderstuff

'Soon' by My Bloody Valentine

'Come Down Softly to My Soul' by Spacemen 3

'Take Me as I Am' by Wyclef Jean featuring Sharissa

'Smooth Operator' by Sade

'Purple Rain' by Prince

Unfortunately things don't always go to plan – just as things start to get very schmoochy, one of the following crops up in the playlist. 'Oh dear,' you think. 'I'll get my coat ...' *No one* can recover from this sort of disaster.

(PART TWO) BANG A GONG

'I'd Do Anything for Love (But I Won't Do That)' by Meat Loaf

'Viva Espana' by Hanna Ahroni

'The Theme from Dambusters' by The Band of the Coldstream Guards

'Mr Hanky the Christmas Poo' by Chef from *South Park*

'Heaven Knows I'm Miserable Now' by The Smiths

'Kill You' by Eminem

'You're So Vain' by Carly Simon

'I'm Your Man' as performed by Shane Ritchie, obviously

'Can We Fix It?' by Bob the Builder

'Bohemian Rhapsody' by Queen

'I Wanna F*** a Dog in the A$$' by Blink-182

The Eleven Greatest Musical Climaxes

Ooh? Aah? In these songs there is, as Gina G so succinctly put it, just a little bit . . .

'Je t'aime . . . moi non plus' by Serge Gainsbourg and Jane Birkin
Released in (19)69, this song about coming and going between your kidneys is, of course, the Mona Lisa of musical orgasms.

'Je t'aime . . . moi non plus' by Serge Gainsbourg and Brigitte Bardot
Jane, though, wasn't the first to succumb to Serge's 'Let's do a duet' routine. Brigitte Bardot, however, sounds a little bored in this, the original version. Her husband wasn't that chuffed either, so her take was canned.

'Orgasm' by Prince
The album is called *Come*, the song is called 'Orgasm'; it's not about saving the whale. Prince teases with his guitar, the lucky lady responds, and there's the sound of waves crashing on a beach to finish things off. Nice.

'French Kiss' by L'il Louis
This late-eighties dance classic beeps along quite nicely until, three and a half minutes in, for absolutely no reason whatsoever, someone proceeds to thoroughly enjoy themselves.

'Love to Love You Baby' by Donna Summer
Donna 'feels' love for a full sixteen minutes and forty-eight seconds. Later sampled by Beyoncé for the appropriately titled 'Naughty Girl'.

'Social Disease' by Bon Jovi
So maybe *Slippery When Wet* isn't about difficult driving conditions after all. The social disease in question is, apparently, the young having a good old time, as epitomized by the short, sharp shag at the beginning of the song.

'En Melody' by Serge Gainsbourg
No Jane or Brigitte on Serge's 1971 classic album *Histoire de Melody Nelson*. Whoever Melody is, Serge provides . . . and she has a particularly saucy attack of the giggles.

'Relax' by Frankie Goes to Hollywood
As Mike Read so brilliantly deduced, this song isn't about unwinding with a nice cup of tea. But does someone actually 'do it'? There are so many 'huh's it's difficult to tell, but on the balance of probability, we say *oh yes*.

'The Balled of 32' by Frankie Goes to Hollywood
However, there's no doubt about this, which puts paid to any suggestion that it's meant to be 'Ballad' on the sleeve.

'Welcome to the Jungle' by Guns N' Roses
Axl wants to hear somebody 'scream'. Somebody helpfully obliges.

'Je t'aime . . . moi non plus' by Frankie Howerd and June Whitfield
A more British take on all things French. Don't tell Terry.

Michael Jackson's Eleven Ways to Make Your Career go 'Pop'

Picture the scene: you are the biggest black child pop star in the history of the world ever and become the biggest white adult pop star in the world ever. Here is what *not* to do next . . .

Say things like . . .

'When I was young, the people I watched were the real showmen – James Brown, Sammy Davis Jr, Fred Astaire, Gene Kelly. A great showman touches everybody.' Allegedly.

Sleep with children

Among his favourite pastimes Jackson lists water-balloon fights with children, climbing trees and sleepovers. He emphasizes that children need and deserve lots of love – not sexual love, but things like having hot milk and cookies, being tucked in and told a bedtime story, etc.

Pay a thirteen-year-old boy millions of dollars

In 1993, a thirteen-year-old boy filed a complaint in which he made certain allegations. Jackson settled the boy's civil lawsuit with the payment of an undisclosed amount of money and the boy declined to testify. This settlement was in no way an admission of guilt.

Get arrested for alleged lewd or lascivious acts

In November 2003, Jackson was booked and released on bail after voluntarily returning to California to face charges of 'lewd or lascivious acts' with a child under fourteen.

Organize a 'Michael is Innocent' rally

Organized by fans, a series of public vigils to protest his innocence were held on 20 November 2003. Not many people turned up. It didn't look good.

Forget to get your private jet swept for bugs

Someone tried to sell secret recordings from a bugged private jet that was chartered to take Jacko and his attorney from Vegas to California.

Forget to hide your alleged porn stash

The uncle of a child who accused Jackson of molestation has made public allegations stating that during the original sex scandal there were hardcore pornographic tapes depicting children found in Jackson's home.

Invite Martin Bashir into your home

Ever.

Be formally charged with sex crimes

On 18 December 2003, Jackson was charged with seven counts of child molestation and two counts of 'administering an intoxicating agent to commit that felony' in February and March that year; all concerned the same boy, who was under fourteen.

Complain about a dirty bathroom
A friend of Jackson's claimed that the star was manhandled by police during his arrest and worst of all that he was locked in a dirty bathroom for more than forty-five minutes. Alone.

Decide to make a film about children 'riding you'
Jackson has plans to make a movie called *Hot Rod* in which he would have the ability to transform into a car which his co-star – an as-yet-uncast adolescent male companion – would ride all over the world. You couldn't make this up.

Easy as ABC, really.

Eleven Prince 'Wash Your Hands' Moments

He may be a Jehovah's Witness these days, but Prince has not always led the Holy life. Not if these following songs are anything to go by . . .

'Gett Off'
There are, of course, the twenty-three positions in the chorus. There's Prince politely commenting on the size of a lady's posterior and generously offering to help with her 'zipper'. But best of all there's the proposed session on the pool table, to involve a different form of cue action. Not to mention an unconventional suggestion about where the eight ball should end up.

'Rock Hard in a Funky Place'
Smarter readers may have a rough idea of which funky place it is that Prince is referring to. But everyone should be heartened by his environmental instincts to drive down waste, even if the particular waste that Prince detests is of the rock-hard variety.

'If I Was Your Girlfriend'
A bit of a psychological one here – or, in the chapter parlance, a head-fuck. Basically Prince imagines what it would be like to be his girlfriend's girlfriend. This involves undressing, washing and philosophizing on the fact that making love and having an orgasm don't have to go together. Oddly, the single edit faded before they got to that bit.

'Alphabet Street'
Funky turns spunky in the middle eight with Prince announcing that, for all his teasing talk about driving to Tennessee, he's not actually in the mood this evening. Instead, he has a different proposal. He'd like to watch. Cat, his dancer/rapper, has other ideas. She would like her lover to (for want of a better word) 'jack' his body in the style of a 'horny pony'. Ahem.

'Horny Toad'
Not to suggest that the pony has the animal monopoly on horniness. Not when Prince and his toads are still around. Hmm.

'Le Grind'
A new dance that, according to Prince, is sweeping the nation. Do we really need to spell out the moves?

'Soft and Wet'
Put it this way, it's not about Andrex puppies left out in the rain.

'Head'
And this isn't about eighties sportswear manufacturers.

'Bambi'
Not so much a homage to a cartoon deer as a homage to a cartoon dear who has a preference for other cartoon dears. This doesn't put his Purpleness off, though – he generously offers to show her why a man, or at least a Prince, will give her a better time.

'Sexy Dancer'
Prince extols the virtues of a particularly hot groover. So hot are her moves that Prince is, in his own immortal words, 'creaming'.

'Sister'
To summarize the lyrics: Prince is sixteen, his sister is thirty-two; she is 'loose'; he can't say no. Enough already.

Eleven AC/DC Dirty Deeds

For those about to innuendo, we salute you . . .

'Let Me Put My Love Into You'
If you want a slice of cake, the boys are generously on hand with a knife. Or should we say, 'knife'.

'Giving the Dog a Bone'
It's not about a dog. And it's not about a bone.

'Beating Around the Bush'
And we're not sure this one is about topiary, either.

'Big Balls'
AC/DC have balls, apparently. And guess what? They're big.

'Love at First Feel'
The 'DC are worried about the age of their most recent conquest. But not *that* worried.

'Sink the Pink'
Not quite the Matchroom Mob featuring Chas and Dave.

'Go Down'
Ruby (verse one) and Mary (verse two) offer the boys a spot of lip service. The boys thank the Lord they are male.

'Girls Got Rhythm'
In sitting terms we're talking backseat rather than the drum stool.

'First Blood'
Put it this way, it's not a homage to Rambo.

'Put the Finger on You'
It's a finger that can, ahem, unlock doors.

'Deep in the Hole'
Now that's just unpleasant.

Eleven Songs about Penises

With phallic guitars, mike stands and 'mine is bigger than yours' amps, it is no surprise that there are so many songs about . . . You know, *down there*.

'Detachable Penis' by King Missile
The lyric is a sweeping and at times querulous one debating the relative values of having a detachable penis and . . . Well, not having one, we suppose.

'The Penis Song' by Monty Python
Who can forget sitting through *The Meaning of Life* with one's parents, expecting ninety minutes of silly walks and finding oneself confronted by a little number Eric Idle had 'tossed off this morning'? Hmm.

'Your Mother's Got a Penis' by Goldie Lookin' Chain
Where does that leave your dad? Chavtastic.

'Pony the Penis' by James Kochalka Superstar
This comes from the seminal album *Hot Rod Monkey*, which also includes other interesting-sounding tracks, such as 'Bathroom Buddies', 'Punch The Clock' and 'Ballbuster'.

'Hooker with a Penis' by (the brilliantly named) Tool
Sort of 'Lola' with balls?

'Gimme Excitation' by Eric and the Erections
Puerile, sniggerworthy and spot on.

'My Ding-a-Ling' by Chuck Berry
The same Chuck Berry caught secretly videotaping women in the bathroom of his restaurant.

'Penis Dimension' by Frank Zappa and the Mothers of Invention
Frank worries here that he doesn't quite, um, 'measure up'.

'Monster' by Fred Schneider
When active his monster has the ability to cause people around it to start shouting.

'Sledgehammer' by Peter Gabriel
There is no evidence to suggest that Pete spent any time involved in the building trade, so it is likely that his exposure to literal sledgehammers is negligible. This lack of hard evidence (sorry) does open up the possibility that Pete's 'sledgehammer' might, just might, be figurative . . .

Various by Tom Green
He deserves a category of his own but suffice it to say he has recorded countless songs about genitalia, including the classics 'The Vagina Song', 'Feel Your Balls' and 'Pet Names for a Penis'. Modesty forbids us reprinting any of the lyrics but, with your mouse in one hand and this book in the other, Google will show you the way.

Eleven Odes to Onanism

Here are a handful of songs that let your fingers do the walking . . .

'Dirty Dream Number 2' by Belle and Sebastian
From the delightful album *The Boy with the Arab Strap* (don't ask).

'Pictures of Lily' by The Who
Their *Meaty Beaty Big and Bouncy* track.

'I Touch Myself' by The Divinyls
Leaves nothing to the imagination.

'Stroke' by Billy Squier
Apparently this is not about cardiac malfunction.

'Under the Pink' by Tori Amos
Ms Amos has written more songs about her ladies' parts than we have typed the word 'eleven' for this volume. We have plumped for this one, which is definitely not about snooker. Oh no.

'Touch of My Hand' by Britney Spears
This was written when the lovely Britney was refusing to let anyone else's hand touch her.

'Ten Little Fingers' by The Who
Back again . . .

'Oops (Oh My)' by Tweet (featuring Missy 'Misdemeanor' Elliott)
Whether Missy Elliott is responsible for the 'Oops' or simply the 'Oh My' is unclear.

'Darling Nikki' by Prince and the Revolution
We didn't know that women did *that* in hotel foyers.

'She Bop' by Cyndi Lauper
Obviously girls just wanna have fun . . . Alone.

'Dancing with Myself' by Billy Idol
Billy's euphemism for pocket billiards is rather sweet – not for him such rubbish as 'straining the potatoes' or 'spanking the monkey'. Bless.

Eleven Groupies have their Say

Picture the scene: you are on stage before a capacity crowd, playing the final song; 15,000 beautiful people sing along and scream and shout, the fireworks explode and you walk off hands aloft.

What do you do next?
a) Say goodbye to the rest of the band, thank them for a lovely evening and tell them you will see them at the next venue.
b) Ring your mum, tell her it went well and ask if she'll leave the front door unlocked for you as you might go for a pizza – though you'll try to be back by eleven and, yes, you'll bring the cat in.
c) Get your head of security to round up fifteen assorted babes, buy an industrial quantity of class-As and head to the after-show, then the hotel lobby, then the suite for a night of coming down . . . Slowly. Form an orderly queue, please.

During our extensive research (i.e., checking out some very dodgy websites) we amassed some verdicts on the following rock stars from some very naughty girls. Can you match the names to the descriptions? If you can you are a bad, bad person . . .

The rock stars (in no particular order)
Jon Bon Jovi
Alice Cooper
David Bowie
Fred Durst
R Kelly
Lenny Kravitz
Simon Le Bon
Lemmy
Kid Rock
Axl Rose
Steve Tyler

The Groupies said . . .
1) Is a 'sex god'. And particularly good at oral sex.
2) Is an 'egomaniac' but 'average at best'.
3) Is into 'beautiful brainy people, orgies and videotaping his encounters'.
4) Is 'very sexy' and 'knows how to satisfy a woman' but 'may not be faithful'!
5) Is 'a sexual flop', a 'dead fish', just 'lying there while you do all the work'.

6) Has 'a curved penis' and likes public sex.
7) Is 'very kinky, likes bondage, sex toys, girl-girl sex and videotaping'.
8) Is a raunchy sex symbol but is a triumph of style over content.
9) Is 'wham bam, thank you, ma'am', into orgies, exhibitionism, and other unmentionable stuff.
10) A 'notorious womanizer', an 'unforgettable lover' and an expert at erotic kissing.
11) Is 'overrated' and a 'sexual disappointment'. Sometimes has trouble getting it up. Recently voted one of the 'least sexiest men in music'.

For the answers, hang out in the front row dressed in low-cut 'leisure-wear' and work it out for yourself later.

I'M WITH THE BAND

Eleven Great Bassists

Not so much two cans short of a six-pack as two strings short of being a proper musician . . .

Bootsy Collins
If you want your song to groove from the bottom upwards, then Bootsy is your man. He can also provide his own selection of spangly costumes at no extra cost.

Alex James
The indie bassist par excellence. Or maybe he is a 'cigarette player' with an occasional bass habit.

Adam Clayton
A case of running (bass) before you could walk. For most of the 1980s, Adam was on cruise control – finding a note and sitting on it for five minutes while Bono and Edge did their stuff. But for *Achtung Baby* Adam revealed himself twice: once on the cover and again on the record, as a bassist who really could move in mysterious ways. The result? He pulled Naomi Campbell.

Bill Wyman
For thirty years it seemed as though Bill Wyman and Charlie Watts had a competition running to see which Stone could look the most bored on stage. Not that Bill was bored off it: restaurateur, painter, youth worker . . .

Alex Griffin and Matt Cheslin
These days, it is all *de rigeur* to do away with the bass player (see The White Stripes and Keane). But in the early nineties staffing levels were at an all-time high. Particularly so for Ned's Atomic Dustbin, whose sole contribution to musical history was to have not one but two bass players. It must have seemed a good idea at the time.

Mark King
Level 42's slap-bass virtuoso had a bass whose frets lit up as he played them. He wore his instrument as a wooden bow-tie. He also had his

thumbs insured for a million pounds – which you'd think would be easy money for a kidnapper with a pair of tin snips, but there you go.

Peter Hook
The man who defined how a bass should be worn. If Mark King did it the wrong way by holding it up high, Joy Division's Peter Hook pioneered the right way by lengthening the strap until the bass was, quite literally, as low as it could go.

John Taylor
John Taylor, particularly around 1983, was as cool as a bass player could get, his cheekbones giving Simon Le Bon more than a run for his money. But be warned: give him half a chance and he'd slap bass like there was no tomorrow.

Sid Vicious
Anyone who argues that a bass player is not a proper musician will often cite Sid Vicious as proof that no talent is needed to play the four-string. At least if he was on stage he couldn't throw anything at the band.

Pino Palladino
There are really only two bassist names to drop: Jaco Pastorious and Pino Palladino. The latter gets into this list by virtue of having the better name. It's so great that you can probably drop it into a conversation on any subject and get away with it: 'Yes, I've had the kitchen re-done, put a Pino Palladino oven in . . .'

Lemmy
Guitarists strum chords. Bass players pluck notes. Unless you're the Bass of Spades, in which case you strum chords. Presumably he got it wrong at his first lesson but the teacher was too scared to correct him.

Eleven Great Drummers

What's the difference between a drummer and a drum machine? You only have to punch the information into a drum machine once.

Animal
The ultimate rock 'n' roll drummer. Animal was wasted in the Muppets' theatre band, with few openings for his riotous style and explosive fills on 'Halfway Down the Stairs' and 'Mah-Na Mah-Na'.

Keith Moon

Moon started as he meant to go on in Greenford 1964, turning up to watch The Who play, smashing up the drummer's kit, announcing that he (Dougie Sandon) was 'crap' and he (Moon) was the man for the job. After that, no hotel room was safe.

Scott Halpin

San Francisco, November 1973. Keith Moon took what can only be described as a foolish amount of tranquilizers. Shortly into the set, he was unconscious. Townshend's desperate cry to placate the crowd was to ask if there were any drummers in. Step forward Scott Halpin, a nineteen-year-old from Iowa, who gamely plugged the Moon-sized hole for the rest of the show.

The drummer on the *EastEnders* tune

For all the big names who play to sell-out stadia eight days a week, there is only one drummer whose star turn is heard by an audience of millions three times a week. The style is a little bit Phil Collins, we'll admit, but you can't knock his timing. '*Douph! Douph! Douph-douph douph-douph douph-douph!*' As rhythmic riffs go, this one's a 'Layla'.

Zack Hanson

Hanson. The teenage band who weren't even all teenagers. For playing drums on a number-one record when his feet could hardly reach the pedals, Zack's in.

Clyde Stubblefield

Drummer to the Godfather of Soul – himself a man of many great songs, but none perhaps so influential as Stubblefield's twenty-second-long solo on his early-seventies classic 'Funky Drummer'. This is one of the most sampled breaks ever (150 times and counting).

Tony McCarroll

The original Oasis drummer, quickly dumped for the lighter touch of Alan White. McCarroll is not, in our opinion, the greatest drummer ever to have sat on a stool, but his agricultural style is exactly what the Oasis sound needs. The moment he left was the moment they started going downhill.

John Bonham

The rival to Keith Moon's crown, John 'Bonzo' Bonham's CV includes covering people with baked beans and octopuses, and shoving hot steak-and-kidney pies down photographers' trousers. But, given the thunderous boom of Zeppelin's 'When the Levee Breaks', there's little we can't forgive.

Mick from Chas and Dave

He's put up with being in Chas and Dave for many years, which is worth some sort of medal on its own. But Mick also merits inclusion for being all but unique among drummers by having his own song. In 'Give it Some Stick, Mick', Mick does just that. Did Charlie Watts or John Bonham ever get such royal treatment? Exactly.

Dave Grohl

Our copy-editor says you've got to Grohl with it. Who are we to disagree?

The Fat Boys

What if you could use your own voice to *replicate* the sound of the drums? Enter that classic eighties stalwart the human beatbox, prime proponents of which were The Fat Boys, who were fat as in, well, fat. Complete with finger-clicking, head-nodding and a spraying of saliva, the box of beat was the sound of playground percussionists everywhere.

Eleven Great Keyboardists

The keyboardist has a fundamental problem in how to rock out and sit down at the same time. Here are eleven who did their best to kick the stool away.

Jean-Michel Jarre

Music to do magic tricks to. You can almost hear the pink cloth being pulled away and the gasps at the pair of cooing doves. No, we don't know how he does it either. The tragic explosion of the space shuttle *Challenger* put paid to the planned highlight of his Rendezvous Houston's extravaganza, the saxophone-from-space solo.

Elton John

Forget all the talk about his hair, the most fascinating part of Elton's anatomy are his eyebrows. You watch the next time he plays. They go up and down as he sings, punctuating the music. A welcome bit of light relief during Diana's funeral, that.

Jerry Lee Lewis

Goodness gracious. The original rock 'n' roll star, Jerry 'Great Balls' Lee was one of the first to make more than the most of the accompanying booze, drugs and women. Lewis's problems arose when the press discovered that his wife was his cousin. Oh yes. And she was thirteen.

Nick Rhodes
Nick Rhodes *is* Duran Duran – in style, in philosophy, and in being the only member of the band to have been there throughout, from the Stephen Tin-Tin Duffy beginnings to the just-him-and-Simon-left late nineties.

Sparky
Technically not Sparky, of course, but his Magic Piano. Sparky didn't want to do his piano practice, but was saved by the fact that the Magic Piano stepped in and played himself. Sparky put his feet up; the Magic Piano got a bit tetchy and wouldn't play. There's a message in there somewhere.

Rick Wakeman
It's a special kind of keyboardist whose masterpiece was a prog version of the King Arthur story. On ice. In one epic battle scene there was one knight too many – it took the hapless warrior a good five minutes of despondent skating before he did the decent thing and fell on his own sword.

Harold Faltermeyer
If the eighties were the keyboard's high point, then Harold Faltermeyer was its Casio king. 'Axel F', the theme song to the original *Beverly Hills Cop*, is about as pure keyboard as a single is able to get. Great for magicians, too.

Mags
A-ha's keyboard pilot is a true pioneer. The only example in musical history of the guitarist (Pal) being the geek and the keyboard player being the good-looking one.

John Lennon, Paul McCartney, Ringo Starr, Mal Evans and George Martin
The five people responsible for the greatest piano chord of all time, the one at the end of 'A Day in the Life'. Played on three pianos and multi-tracked four times, this chordal whopper (an E) quite simply rings out like no other.

Max Rebo
Arguably the greatest keyboardist in the galaxy, Max Rebo was the driving force behind Jabba the Hutt's house (or should that be palace?) band. A sort of sci-fi blue elephant, Max came from the planet Orto and, like all keyboard players, had an ear for music and a stomach for food.

Tim Rice-Oxley
Frankie from The Darkness describes Keane as 'more sheet-soilers than bedwetters and play music to suck your thumb to'. But credit where

credit's due: to get away without a bassist is one thing; to get away without a bassist and a guitarist is quite another. For that, young Tim on piano, we salute you.

Eleven Unlikely Guest Appearances on Record

Mick Jagger on 'You're So Vain' by Carly Simon
Mick Jagger's undeniable presence on the session suggests that either a) it's *not* about him or b) he's got an otherwise undocumented sense of humour. The only two clues about its real target we have are a) it's not about James Taylor and b) she once assured Dick Ebersol, president of NBC sports, that the subject's name contains the letter 'e'. It cost poor Dick $50,000 to find that out. We're telling you for less than a tenner!

Phil Collins on 'Puss in Boots' by Adam Ant
When asked why a frivolous panto-rock band would have recruited a dour old prog-jazz type, Adam Ant said: 'Phil is a great drummer. He had a great drum sound – doosh – and I got it.' Phil's mighty tub-thumping also underpins the single's B-side, 'Kiss the Drummer'. Forgive us if we don't.

The Average White Band on 'My Ding-A-Ling' by Chuck Berry
In 1972, a flurry of interest in the original rock 'n' rollers brought (among others) Chuck Berry to the UK. His current album featured songs recorded at the Lanchester Arts Festival where Chuck was second on the bill to Pink Floyd – who were trying out songs from *Dark Side of the Moon*. On that fateful night, when Chuck recorded his only UK number one, The Average White Band's ill-fated drummer, Robbie McIntosh, and their second guitarist, Onnie McIntyre, were among his backing band.

Elton John on the *Young Guns II* soundtrack by Jon Bon Jovi
Not just Elton but also Jeff Beck and Little Richard guest on Jon's 1990 album spin-off from the Brat Pack Western. The vocals are a little high in the mix – rendering the words somewhat more comprehensible than they really merit.

Billy Joel on 'Leader of the Pack' by The Shangri-La's
Billy Joel is definitely not the luckiest man in showbusiness. He was the victim of the all-time classic rip-off (a contract with Ripp productions cost him a percentage of his royalties for nearly twenty years), and he was

never paid for playing on one of the all-time classic pop songs, 'Leader of the Pack', because he wasn't a Musicians' Union member.

Herb Alpert on 'Rat in Mi Kitchen' by UB40
UB40's song of rodent infestation – the signature tune of every environmental-health inspector in the UK – is one of Herb's many guest appearances on other people's records. Today Mr Alpert is best known for his *Whipped Cream & Other Delights* album – mainly because of the lady on the cover, Dolores Erickson.

Sting on 'Money for Nothing' by Dire Straits
The song that, perhaps more than any other, says, 'MTV'. In fact, more than any other, this song also says, 'I want my. . .' Initially Mark Knopfler didn't credit Sting, who just happened to be passing the volcano-prone Air recording studios in Montserrat and popped in to add some extra vocals. His publishers swiftly pointed out that they echo the melody of the Police hit 'Don't Stand So Close to Me'.

Ray Stevens on 'Sugar Sugar' by The Archies
The Archies were, of course, an entirely imaginary group, masterminded by bubblegum overlord Ron Dante. There was once a playground rumour that Ray Charles had dropped in to provide handclaps on 'Sugar Sugar', but the truth is that they were the work of the entirely more plausible Ray 'The Streak' Stevens.

Stevie Wonder on 'Lovin' You' by Minnie Riperton
Contractual problems forbade Stevie from appearing on anyone else's records at the time, so the production of Minnie's *Perfect Angel* album was credited to Wonderlove (Stevie's backing band) and the keyboards, drums and harmonica to a mysterious figure known only as El Toro Negro.

Donovan on 'Yellow Submarine' by The Beatles
Unlike most of the Ringo-sung songs, this sort of works. Donovan was travelling with The Beatles on their Indian trip in 1967; he suggested some lyric changes while Paul was writing the song and then took part in the background chorus of the recording. Paul returned the favour with a guest appearance on 'Mellow Yellow' in the same year.

George Harrison on 'Badge' by Cream
Cream's Eric Clapton was a close pal of George – they even shared a girlfriend for a while, back in the sixties. The title of this song, depending on which interview you read, is either the chords of the song (B-A-D-G-E) or Eric's misreading of the word 'bridge' inscribed on the working lyric

sheet by Harrison. Why *was* George credited as L'Angelo Mysterioso when everyone knew it was him?

Eleven Great Backing Singers

Sometimes they can sing. Sometimes they're just the singer's girlfriend.

Pepsi and Shirlie
Peps and Shirl wiggled strangely on *The Pops* as George and Andrew tried to impress them with their shuttlecocks down their pants. Not that they were there as a beard for George's sexuality or anything. They went on to score a couple of Top Ten hits – precisely two more than Andrew.

Lorraine McIntosh
Deacon Blue's secret weapon was the girlfriend of singer Ricky Ross and an expert at making train noises ('Wooh-wooh!'). Ricky would sing a line, then Lorraine would repeat it, louder and higher. And slightly less in tune.

Sheryl Crow
In 1988, Sheryl was a backing singer for Michael Jackson on his big Bad tour. Despite a frightwig of bedwetting proportions and having to wear one of Michael's ridiculous costumes, Sheryl attracted the unwanted attention of Michael's manager, Frank Dileo. Revenge, served cold, appeared on Sheryl's debut album, where she discussed said Mr Dileo's 'dong'.

Patti Sciafla
The most expensive backing singer in musical history. Patti Sciafla had the flowing red locks and the tambourine-tapped-against-thigh routine down pat, all too much for her boss, The Boss, to resist. Mrs Springsteen, unsurprisingly, was none too chuffed, and in the subsequent divorce stung her husband for a walloping $20 million. Ouch.

Linda McCartney
Poor old Linda. The press never quite forgave her for not being Jane Asher. Less the star than the Starr of Wings, the Moll of Kintyre's legacy was sealed by the circulation of a tape taken off the mixing desk of a live concert, isolating her particularly out-of-tune vocal contribution. An album of Linda songs released following her death suggested that this was misrepresentative, though Heather Mills has yet to be invited on stage.

Joanne Catherall and Susanne Sulley
In 1980, Phil Oakey went to the Crazy Daisy nightclub and found himself two seventeen-year-old girls to join The Human League as backing singers. The other band members weren't always complimentary ('Susanne flails about like an octopus and Joanne's completely out of tune,' said one), but the girls' pouty twist was exactly what the band needed. By 1986, there were only the three of them left.

Helen Terry
The fifth member of Culture Club. While Boy's understanding of pop helped to bring the band both publicity and prominence, it was Helen Terry's huge voice that gave tunes such as 'Church of the Poison Mind' that all-important bit of soul.

Dee C Lee
Did it for The Style Council. Having had a fantastically rhyming name – three times over! – Dee spoilt it slightly by getting married to Paul Weller.

The Glastonbury Festival crowd, 2002
Playing their breakthrough hit, 'Yellow', Coldplay singer Chris Martin decided to hand over vocal duties to the audience. The result was what is known in the business as a 'moment'.

Adam Clayton, Bono, Bob Geldof, Johnny Fingers, Simon Crowe, Pete Briquette, Holly Johnson, Midge Ure, Chris Cross, Simon Le Bon, Nick Rhodes, Andy Taylor, John Taylor, Roger Taylor, Paul Young, Tony Hadley, Martin Kemp, John Keeble, Gary Kemp, Steve Norman, Martyn Ware, Glenn Gregory, Francis Rossi, Rick Parfitt, Sting, Boy George, John Moss, Marilyn, Keren Woodward, Sarah Dallin, Siobhan Fahey, Jody Watley, Paul Weller, Robert 'Kool' Bell, James Taylor, Dennis Thomas and George Michael
Was there ever a more star-studded line-up of backing singers than Band Aid?

Bananarama
They started off doing backing vocals for The Professionals and Department S. Then it was the turn of Fun Boy Three. And, though Bananarama graduated on to having hits of their own, they remain for our money backing singers in all but name. Even one of their biggest hits, 'Na Na Hey Hey (Kiss Him Goodbye)', sounds like the backing vocals for someone else's song.

Eleven Rock Children

Grace Slick and Paul Kantner: China
There is a long-standing urban legend that the Jefferson Airplane pair named their firstborn 'god', but that's based on a joke Grace made while still delirious from labour and medication. When a nurse asked the new mother what her baby's name was going to be, she joked, 'god. We spell it with a small g because we want her to be humble.' In truth, the little girl was always called China. That's *loads* better.

Frank Zappa: Dweezil, Moon Unit Two, Ahmet, and Diva Muffin
When it was suggested to Frank that his offspring might not thank him for his eccentric name choices he insisted that they would have more trouble carrying the surname Zappa through life. It's the kind of logic that would have us putting out fires with petrol.

John Cougar Mellencamp and Elaine Irwin: Speck Wildhorse
To name one's son after a sort of ham seems like the worst kind of folly. Young Speck could have had the piss taken at school with a name like that. Fortunately, his mum is a top swimwear model, so he's probably OK.

David and Angie Bowie: Zowie
The classic silly rock name – chosen, it seems, purely for its consonance with Bowie's adopted surname. Once he was old enough, Zowie wasted little time in changing his name to the rather more dignified Joe Heywood Jones.

Billy Ray Cyrus: Destiny Hope
Although no evidence exists that the be-mulleted 'Achy Breaky Heart' singer was a big fan of Captain Scarlet, his choice of name for his daughter does suggest a certain familiarity with the invulnerable wooden mysteron-basher. Destiny uses her nickname, Miley, for her acting career. Her dad thought that one up, too.

Buffy Sainte-Marie: Dakota Star Blanket Wolfchild
It's arguable that Sainte-Marie's son's name is a list of the first things she saw after he was born, as per Cherokee tradition – but then wouldn't Dakota's name be Nurse Flower-Shop Bedpan?

Smokey Robinson: Berry and Tamla
You can't fault Smokey's loyalty: he named his son after his record-label owner and his daughter after the label itself. At least Tamla sounds a *bit* like a name. Imagine Vertigo Robinson.

Michael Jackson: Prince Michael, Prince Michael II, Paris Michael
We weren't expecting rational choices from Old Vinyl-Head, but they're *all* called Michael? Please!

Gary Numan: Raven
We like Gary: he can fly, he gives good quote, and he's got a great wig. Chillingly, Gary Numan is thirteen days *older* than Gary Oldman.

The Edge: Blue Angel
Dissolute Dietrich drama? Or US Air Force display team? We'll never know . . .

Michael Hutchence and Paula Yates: Heavenly Hiraani Tiger Lily
Still only eight, she hasn't yet dropped that great weight of a name, but we sort of hope she does. She was adopted aged four by Sir Bob in one of those irrepressible acts of decency we love the old fella for, no matter how bad his records get.

Eleven Great Dancers

Any fool can play an instrument, but only they can do *that*.

Stacia
Statuesque, naked, dazzle-painted to deter U-Boats, she was Hawkwind's secret weapon. When they made her wear a swimsuit on *Top of the Pops*, she still made a generation of young boys feel all peculiar.

Chas Smash
When you see this Madness hero, you know immediately that all the key skills are there: he can do the nutty dance, wear an apron or a hat with equal aplomb, and can, when required, hold a trumpet. An asset to any ska ensemble.

Bez
If you ever saw The Happy Mondays live, you might know that feeling when Bez's 1,000-yard stare swept over the audience like drugged-up Nazi searchlights and came to rest on *you*. Was he about to lamp you with those maracas? No, he was just checking that you were 'sorted'; once he was satisfied, his baleful beams would rake the audience once more.

Barry Mooncult

You might be forgiven for seeing double-glazing-fitter Barry as a Bez-come-lately, employed by Flowered Up just to emulate his northern cousin's success. Not so: Barry wore his mum's aerobics gear and a big flower on his head, making him the missing link between Bez and Peter Gabriel.

Jerome Benton

Not strictly a dancer, Jerome is listed as The Time's 'Stage Valet'. He takes care of Morris Day's 'personal' details when the band are performing. The benchmark for all aspiring performance butlers.

Paul Rutherford

Mustachioed, handsome enough to make any straight man think again, and entirely devoid of musical talent – Paul Rutherford is truly the Tom Selleck of rock. If Holly wore an overcoat, Paul wore a vest. If Holly wore a warm jacket, Paul wore a *different* vest. Frankie were like that.

Cat

Prince has never failed to find astounding young women to take part in his funky carnival troupe. *Sign o' the Times*-era dancer Cat boasted a human special effect: she could ricochet around the stage looking like a very sexy piece of beef jerky.

Jed Hoile

As a fairly annoying pop star, Howard Jones knew he would struggle to succeed – but he figured that by the simple expedient of employing a mime artist, everyone's most hated kind of performer, he would appear more likable by contrast. It worked. When Howard phased Jed out of his live shows, the hits dried up.

Kate Moss

Yes, *that* Kate Moss. She lent her gift of looking washed yet still somehow dirty to the White Stripes' Dusty Springfield cover 'I Just Don't Know What to Do with Myself'. Just a few hundred viewings of a fuzzy RealPlayer rendering of her poledancing routine tells us that she probably knows *exactly* what to do with herself.

Jimmy Gulzar

Employed as a dancer by The Spice Girls at the height of their fame, Jimmy 'Goldcard' soon became more than a dancer for Shouty Spice Mel B. Mel became Mel G and the future looked bright. Unfortunately the future was only eighteen months long, after which came a period of bitter recriminations, happy lawyers, and paintings on eBay.

Christopher Walken

Chris was little known as a dancer before his appearance in the 'Weapon of Choice' video for Fatboy Slim. Given that he has the sartorial style of Chas Smash, the grace of Cat and the terrifying eyes of Bez, it seems shocking that he had never been asked to dance in a pop video before. We'll be 'moon-walken' all the way to the TV next time Chris says yes!

Eleven Managers and Moguls

Brian Epstein

With The Beatles, he became not the first but certainly the most successful of a long line of gentlemen in pop with a special understanding for the appeal of pale young boys.

Ricky Gervais

Ricky 'looked after' Suede in their formative years. The band saw him very much as friend first, manager second. Probably entertainer third.

Malcolm McLaren

First for The New York Dolls, and then for The Sex Pistols, Malcolm put his loopy situationist concepts to work in the area of rock-band management. The arrangement didn't work all that well, but no one expected it to. Least of all Malcolm. Despite his complete lack of musical ability, he went on to make two of the best albums of the eighties.

Peter Grant

Led Zeppelin's main man, and chief exponent of the 'manager as an object of terror' methodology. Peter Grant looked like some Viking Bezerker about to cleft someone's head in at least twain, if not more. That's because he was.

Simon Fuller

The man to blame every time a fry-cook decides that he or she ought to be on your television. Singing. Badly. We always love the first couple of episodes of every series of *Whatever Idol*, when the real basket-cases are on, but tend to glaze over once the contenders are pared down to indistinguishable Sylvia Young rejects who do that funny wobbly-chin thing.

Steve Dagger

We're willing to bet that the first thing you'll think when you read Steve's name is 'Wow! What a cool name!' and that the second thing is 'Who?'

Steve is one of the two great Steves of eighties rock-music management – the other is perennial eccentric Stevo – but only Steve Dagger makes our list because, first of all, he managed Spandau Ballet (he gets a prize for that) and secondly, he's *Steve Dagger*.

Ronan Keating
Boyzone's lead weasel also acted as figurehead manager for missed-the-gay-disco-bit-and-went-straight-to-the-long-coat-part Westlife. The two acts are more or less indistinguishable to the untrained eye, but Ronan was skilled enough to know which one to sing for and which one to pretend to manage.

Alan McGee
With few or no assets – £40, an O level in maths, a mane of Titian hair – Alan founded Creation Records, became pals with Tony Blair, and inspired The Pooh Sticks' song 'I Know Someone Who Knows Someone Who Knows Alan McGee Quite Well'. He then disbanded his creation Creation and (creatively) created another creation, Poptones.

Simon Napier-Bell
Simon's lengthy career – taking in The Yardbirds, Marc Bolan and Wham! – is best summarized in his pair of gossipy memoirs. We'll summarize it ourselves anyway: trumpet player, probably had a dalliance with Little Richard, wrote the lyrics to a song, accidentally became a manager. Cracking.

Sharon Osbourne
Daughter of the fearsome Don Arden, Sharon has the ability not only to prevent the perpetually befuddled Ozzy from spilling soup down himself, but also to turn him into a multi-million-dollar industry while she's at it. Comfortably the sweariest mogul on our list.

'Knocker' Knowles
Like Sharon, a graduate of the Don Arden school of no-nonsense management. He was Arden's enforcer during the ELO and Sabbath years, then went on to work for Magnet Records. If you want a recalcitrant A&R man dangled upside-down over a stairwell, the Knocker's your man.

Eleven Great Roadies

These are the special men who keep the machinery of rock running: night after night they change guitar strings, lift Hammond organs and arrange 'special' access for the more attractive autograph-seekers. Here is a list of the eleven greatest. For legal reasons we can't tell you exactly *why* they made it into this chart; just know that they can get you stuff that isn't available via room service.

Pyro Pete (The Rolling Stones)

Kremmen (The Clash/Tina Turner)

The Borga (REO Speedwagon/Cyndi Lauper)

Moke (Spiñal Tap)

Dinky Dawson (Steely Dan)

Mississippi (Little Feat)

Dave 'Blast' Bailey (Bryan Adams)

Pedro and the Bat (Fine Young Cannibals)

'Little Carl' Cornell (The Patti Smith Group/Jeff Beck)

Gimpo (KLF)

Karl 'Special K' Kuenning (Jean-Luc Ponty/The Patti Smith Group)

'Hello, I'm a Film-Maker': Eleven Real-Life Marty DiBergis

Neil Young, *Rust Never Sleeps* (1979)
He played the concert and he directed the movie. It saves on backstage passes.

Martin Scorsese, *The Last Waltz* (1978)
Don Simpson said of a young Scorsese in the seventies: 'He had this rock 'n' roll head, knew every lyric and every title. He understood that the music was really a critical aspect of the zeitgeist of the times.' That might explain the success of this rockumentary about The Band's farewell concert, but leaves us wondering how come he auditioned Neil Diamond for *Taxi Driver*?

D. A. Pennebaker, *Don't Look Back* (1967)
A real specialist in the field – as well as this Dylan-on-the-road classic, Pennebaker has shot concert movies for groundbreakers like Jimi Hendrix, David Bowie, and . . . Depeche Mode!

Anton Corbijn, *Depeche Mode: One Night in Paris - Exciter Tour 2001*
Best known as a stills photographer, Anton has also directed a Captain Beefheart movie. We have no idea what that might be like. Then again, we have no idea how to pronounce Anton's surname.

Adrian Maben, *Pink Floyd: Live at Pompeii* (1972)
He describes his Pink Floyd concert movie as an 'anti-Woodstock'. Maybe because there's no audience, maybe because it didn't last three days.

Michael Wadleigh, *Woodstock* (1969)
Michael's directed only two movies – *Woodstock* and a frankly rather weird horror caper called *Wolfen*. He's currently working as a bus driver in Akron, Ohio.

Peter Clifton and Joe Massot, *The Song Remains the Same* (1976)
It took two directors to make a mess of this: a terrible concert by Led Zeppelin, the greatest live attraction of their day.

Murray Lerner, *Isle of Wight Festival 1970*
Murray's responsible for all kinds of craziness: Sci-fi B-movies, Westerns, and a weird 3-D kids 'n' kites affair for Disney. Filming Keith Emerson killing his organ must've seemed like just another day at the office for dear old Muz.

Gavin Taylor, *Queen: Live at Wembley Stadium* (1986)
Gavin specializes in the theatrical: as well as capturing Queen at the height of their powers he shot the *Les Miserables* DVD. Just as long as he's not tempted into immortalizing that Ben Elton Queen show *We Will Rock You*, we'll carry on liking him.

Nick Wickham, *The Red Hot Chili Peppers: Live at Slane Castle* (1992)
A truly classic concert movie – even surpassing U2's show at the same venue. They play a Ramones song! Flea plays the trumpet!

David Mallett, *AC/DC: Live at Donington*
No, not David *Mamet*, he's *far* too brainy. This is David Mallett. He does a lot of concert movies. And *Riverdance*, God help him.

Eleven Rock Wives

It's comparatively easy to become a groupie, even today. The step up to 'girlfriend' status isn't *so* hard, but to be a rock wife takes some doing. Unless you meet Rod Stewart.

Meg Matthews
She came, she saw, she maxed out the credit card.

Patsy Kensit
One of the great rock wives: Jim Kerr *and* Liam Gallagher.

Priscilla Presley
Pris's policy? If you're going to marry only one rock 'n' roll star, make it the best.

David Furnish
All right, not *strictly* a wife, but he's always dressing Elton up as wallpaper so we think he's funny enough to make it.

Angie Bowie
Not just Dave, but also one of The New York Dolls and then Marianne Faithfull. She could write a book! Oh. She did. Twice.

Bebe Buell
Miss November '74. Girlfriend to Todd Rundgren, Mick Jagger, Steven Tyler, Elvis Costello, David Bowie and Jimmy Page . . . But she *married* Coyote Shivers. Who?

Jerry Hall
To her credit, she stuck with the same husband and haircut long after they ceased to be fashionable.

Courtney Love
The Yoko of grunge. Got to the 'girlfriend' stage with an even dozen musicians you'll have heard of, but married Kurt Cobain – thereby alienating every check-shirt owner in the continental US.

Paula Yates
We all know about the marriage to Bob Geldof, the eccentric child-naming policy, and the tragic comedy of the Hutchence years – but did you know that she once tickled one of these authors? He ran away.

Mandy Smith

Encouraged by her mother to date forty-seven-year-old Bill Wyman when she was only thirteen, given a record deal by Pete Waterman, married said Rolling Stone, married a footballer, fêted by the tabloids and then forgotten. Had her mum indeed married Bill Wyman's son, as she was rumoured to have done at the time, Mandy would also have become her mother's stepmother.

Chrissie Hynde

She *tried* to marry Ray Davies, but was refused a licence because they argued so much in the registry office. Later married Simple Minds' intro specialist Jim Kerr. As a major rock talent herself she doesn't really count, but we liked the registry-office story too much to ignore it.

MEDIA WHORES

The Eleven Best Rock 'n' Roll Slogans and Catchphrases

In a media-savvy world, rock 'n' roll is not immune from an advertising or identity-defining slogan. 'You can't get better than a fit Rik Witter' just missed out at number twelve . . .

'Stop the traffic, rock and roll' (U2)
Rattle and Hum time from Bono and the boys. The band played 'All Along the Watchtower'; Bono climbed a statue and sprayed. The traffic responded by saying, 'Stop the rock and roll.'

'Italians do it better' (Madonna)
Seen on a T-shirt worn in the 'Papa Don't Preach' vid. Madonna was born in Michigan.

'4 Real' (The Manic Street Preachers)
Steve Lamacq questioned Richey's authenticity in an interview. Richey sliced his arm up for proof.

'God' (Eric Clapton)
In the cream of Eric's career, London's walls were forever pestered with graffiti proclaiming his deity status. But if he really was all-powerful, wouldn't he have had Hendrix nobbled?

'Slave' (Prince)
That's 'Slave' as in multi-millionaire with a whopping great contract he wants to get out of. Prince pencilled it on his cheek.

'Dave' (Blur)
That's 'Dave' as in Britpop drummer pricking Prince's pomposity by cheekily following suit.

'Cool as fuck' (The Inspiral Carpets)
They weren't, were they?

'Relax' (Frankie Goes to Hollywood)
The T-shirt of nineteen-eighty-phwoar.

'There ain't no party like an S Club party' (S Club 7)
They never invited us, so we don't know. Probably just as well, though –
apart from Rachel, we can't remember any of their names.

'James' (James)
Compulsory late-eighties student T-shirt, with 'Ja' on the front, 'm' on the
side and 'es' on the back.

'For those about to rock (we salute you)' (AC/DC)
Salutes you, too, sirs.

Eleven Great Books by Rock Celebrities

What they really wanted was to be paperback writers. And they were . . .

Tarantula by Bob Dylan
If you don't understand 'Visions of Johanna', don't even bother opening
the cover.

The Beautiful Losers by Leonard Cohen
Laugh-out-loud romantic comedy with a happy ending. Possibly.

Lord Iffy Boatrace by Bruce Dickinson
In a word, iffy.

Goodnight Steve McQueen by Louise Wener
What the lead singer from Sleeper did next. You've been up all night
worrying about that, haven't you?

And the Ass Saw the Angel by Nick Cave
An inbred child born dumb and acutely sensitive. Another gag-fest,
then.

Blackbird Singing: The Poems and Lyrics 1965–1999 by Paul
McCartney
We think he's saving 'The Frog Chorus' for Volume Two.

The English Roses by Madonna
Shockingly shock-free children's book.

Lifehouse by Pete Townshend
Pinball wizard turns keyboard wizard.

Awaydays by Kevin Sampson
Former manager of The Farm in quite-good-novel shocker.

Crucfiy Me Again by Mark Manning
Zodiac Mindwarp. Print Mover.

A Mother's Gift by Britney Spears
Brit-lit, with a little help from Mum.

Eleven Great Rock and Pop Tabloid Headlines

Very, very occasionally, a pop star does something that ends up on the front page of a tabloid newspaper. Strange, we know, but true. Here are a few of our favourites.

'The Filth and the Fury!'
It's the exclamation mark we particularly like in the *Daily Mirror*'s shock-and-outrage coverage of The Sex Pistols swearing on telly.

'Wacko Jacko'
Was this 1986 *Sun* headline where the moniker began? What seemed particularly wacko to the newspaper was his £85,000 'oxygen-filled' bed/test-tube.

'Kick this Evil Bastard Out!'
The *Daily Star* extends a warm hand of welcome to Snoop Doggy Dogg.

'Atomic Splitten'
The *Sun* reveals that the girl group will never be whole again. A nation turns to page two.

'Zip Me Up Before You Go Go'
George Michael. A public toilet. A good-looking policeman.

'Pop Idols Sneer at Dying Kids'
The Beastie Boys not quite the *Daily Mirror*'s favourite band. The *Daily Mirror* not quite The Beasties' paper of record.

'Mystery of Elton's Silent Dogs'
'RSPCA probe shock claim that they had their barks removed,' claimed the *Sun*. It was the *Sun*, however, who was barking.

'Who Breaks a Butterfly on a Wheel?'
William Rees-Mogg's sixties-defining *Times* editorial in defence of Mick Jagger.

'Public Eminem No. 1'
Their name is, their name is the *Daily Mail*.

'Spliff Club Seven'
So *that*'s why there ain't no party . . .

'Elvis is Alive'
And the *Sunday Sport* have the pictures to prove it.

The Eleven Worst Radio DJs

Last night a DJ saved my life. This morning a DJ woke me up and annoyed me until I switched the radio off. When Taffy sang 'I Love My Radio', she wasn't including these guys . . .

Bruno Brookes
The 'Smashy and Nicey'-generation DJ who didn't take the hint, who found himself shoved further and further down the schedule, who even when given the graveyard slot, four to seven a.m., still turned up to work. But the biggest radio crime he committed was what is technically known as the barefaced lie. As an impressionable young teenager, one of these authors wrote to Bruno Brookes when he was keeping the teatime seat warm. Bruno read out the letter. Bruno said, and we quote, 'I'll send you a pen in the post, mate.' Did the pen ever arrive? Did it heck.

Mark Goodier
Another DJ full of listener promises, another DJ who did not fulfil them. This time it was our friend who wrote in, got her letter read out on air and was promised a Mark Goodier 'goody jar'. What is in a Mark Goodier goody jar?

Don't ask us, or our friend, because it never turned up. Mark is also famous for holding the shortest-ever tenure of the Radio One breakfast show.

Kevin Greening
Crimes against radio humanity, part one: replacing Mark and Lard on the breakfast show. Crimes against radio humanity, part two: said breakfast show, the Kevin and Zoe show, which was not so much wacky as, well, wack. Who thought Kevin reading the travel news in a funny voice as hilarious character Major Hold Ups was a good idea? Crimes against radio humanity, part three: his 'Joke *du jour*' feature. Here Kevin would read out the set-up to a joke at the end of a show, and deliver the punchline . . . at the start of the next one. Comedy, it's all about timing.

Mike Read
It's not about the poetry. It's not about the pulling out of the acoustic guitar at every given opportunity. It's not about his Cliff musical. It's about the fact that, as Radio One breakfast-show host in the mid-1980s, and thus by definition the man with his finger supposedly on the nation's pulse, he got it wrong about Frankie Goes to Hollywood and smashed their single 'Relax' live on air for being too offensive. Frankie said, 'Relax.' If only Mike had.

Chris Evans
There are several periods of Chris Evans that could be included in this list. There were the later weeks of his Radio One tenure (if it was an ITV show, it would be called *When Good DJs Go Bad*). There was the post-Billie-wedding Virgin Radio slot, when he dispensed with his sidekick team and tried to go it alone. But, for us, the Chris Evans who must be included is the Chris Evans who wasn't there. Radio One had declined to let him have Fridays off, so he'd left; Virgin gave him Fridays off, so once a week we were given the *Chris Evans Breakfast Show* complete with back-room team but missing, er, Chris Evans.

Bruno and Liz
A second entry for Bruno, for his part in perhaps one of the worst radio shows of all time. Together, Bruno and Liz Kershaw (now a perfectly presentable and listenable DJ on 6 Music) hosted a hilarious weekend breakfast show during which they pretended not to get on and shouted at each other. The DJ equivalent of sandpaper on a blackboard.

Alan Partridge
The one-time host of the early-morning breakfast show on Radio Norwich, and a man whose taste in music (REO Speedwagon, Wings) sits nicely beside his fascinating facts and choice opinions. Alan was subsequently

moved to a late-evening slot. His career trajectory looks better only by comparison to that of Dave Clifton, who sank from breakfast-show DJ to the graveyard slot.

Lisa I'Anson
Occasionally, the BBC try to poach a bit of MTV talent to make themselves trendy; Zane Lowe excepted, it never works. Witness Kash on the 'all-new' *Top of the Pops*. And listen to Lisa, with a radio voice two parts foghorn to one part cigarettes. But her finest hour was that in which she said nothing: in Ibiza as part of a Radio One dance weekend, Lisa went partying and didn't turn up for her show. Class.

Dr Fox
A DJ who is, we believe, neither a doctor nor a fox. What can we say? The man bleeds cheese.

Steve Penk
In here to represent that most hilarious of radio types, the prankster. Edmonds may have started the 'funny' phone call, Scott Mills may be the next-generation Noel, but Penky is, we think, the master of the art. Who else could have got through to Tony Blair with a wobbly William Hague impression? Over the years, Penk's pranks have led to a succession of badly judged career moves. For example, as the heir to Chris Tarrant's spot at Capital, he gambled on going to host Virgin's breakfast show; he was sacked within months.

Dave Pearce
Time for the pub.

Eleven Pop Stars who Posed Nude

'We don't have to take our clothes off to have a good time . . .' sang Jermaine Stewart in 1986. You do, though, if you want Hugh Hefner to hand over the cheque.

Blu Cantrell
Blue indeed. Before her 2003 summer smash, 'Breathe', Blu was better known for letting her body do just that.

Madonna
Not so much Madonna with child as Madonna with cat.

Geri Halliwell
Glamour Spice. Too much muscle from swimming to make Page 3.

Samantha Fox
Sam 'Touch Me' Fox, however, had no problem getting in.

LaToya Jackson
Jackson sister turned thriller.

Carmen Electra
Spotted in the early nineties by His Purpleness, who took her on tour as his support act and came up with the touching ballad 'Go-Go Dancer' for her. 'Go-Go' didn't go. *Playboy* phoned instead.

Warren Cuccurollo
Andy Taylor's replacement in Duran Duran sells his 'Rock Rod' over the Internet and goes into porn.

Tiffany
For all boys who think they're alone now, previously teenaged Tiffany returned a decade later to grace the pages of *Playboy*.

Belinda Carlisle
With a new GoGos album to promote, Belinda, too, took up the *Playboy* pound.

Nancy Sinatra
The girl whose boots were made for walking, meanwhile, showed she was holding up well by posing aged fifty-five.

Britney Spears
It hasn't happened yet – but, let's face it, it's only a matter of time.

Eleven Great Rock and Pop TV Swearfests

Live TV. A microphone. A profession with a predilection to shock. It's always going to end in fucking tears.

The Sex Pistols
Queen couldn't make Bill Grundy's *Today* show, so The Pistols were lined up as a last-minute replacement. 'Say something outrageous,' said Grundy.

The Sex Pistols did. Lorry driver James Holmes, forty-seven, was so incensed that he kicked his TV in. Fucking idiot.

Bob Geldof
It's Live Aid. It's Bob looking unsurprisingly knackered after single-handedly organizing an international rock concert. It's what is known as a passionate request for your money.

Shaun Ryder
The man who stopped *TFI Friday* going out live. Like a man with Tourette's, Shaun just couldn't stop the swear words coming out. His version of 'Pretty "Fucking" Vacant' didn't help matters.

Five Star
It's *Going Live*. It's Sarah Greene hosting the phone-in. It's one incisive caller who enquires of the band why they're so fucking crap.

Matt Bianco
It's *Saturday Superstore*. It's Simon Roberts on line one. It's Matt Bianco who are told they are a bunch of wankers.

Madonna
Madge had form, having sworn like a trooper on *David Letterman* many years before. Nevertheless, the live coverage of the Turner Prize was hers to decorate with the phrase 'Right on, motherfucker'.

Pink
The Madge for the twenty-first century let her T-shirt do the talking on *CD:UK*. 'You Fucking Bitch', it said succinctly.

Serge Gainsbourg
Mr Gallic Phallic found himself sat next to Whitney Houston on a chat show. Whitney doesn't speak French. If she did, she'd have understood Serge telling the host how much he'd like to fuck her.

Jools Holland
Squeeze keyboardist turned *Tube* presenter makes an unappreciated comment about 'groovy fuckers' on live TV.

Slash
Quite what they were doing inviting him on to Saturday-morning TV, God only knows. Slash told the kids a touching story about an iguana that bit the fuck out of him.

Ozzy Osbourne
'F***, f***, f***, Sharon. F*** . . .'
    Et cetera.

Eleven 'As Seen on TV' Moments

Top of the Pops. The Tube. The Old Grey Whistle Test. Cheggers Plays Pop.
Some bands are just meant to steal the show . . .

Jimi Hendrix performing 'Sunshine of Your Love'
On *The Lulu Show* in 1968, Hendrix crunched 'Hey Joe' to an end,
announced his disappointment at Cream splitting up and proceeded to
perform an incendiary and tributary version of their classic.

Frankie Goes to Hollywood performing 'Relax'
It was early 1983, it wasn't the definitive version, but it was enough for
Trevor Horn to sign them and spend the rest of year working out how to
wind up Mike Read.

The Stone Roses trying to perform 'Made of Stone'
In 1989, in a moment of solid elevenness, the band were too loud for *The
Late Show's* system and fused the electrics. Presenter Tracy McCleod did
her best to fill in. Ian Brown wandered around in the background
shouting, 'Amateurs . . . Amateurs . . . We're wasting our time here, lads.'

Nirvana performing 'Smells Like Teen Spirit'
Kurt Cobain treated his 1991 *Top of the Pops* audience to a low, mumbly
version of the song.

PiL performing 'Rise'
John Lydon, meanwhile, was meant to mime during his 1986 *Top of the
Pops* appearance. He couldn't really be arsed.

Elvis Presley on the '68 *Comeback Special*
The pelvis was back, and he'd discovered black leather.

Madonna, Britney and Christina performing 'Like a Virgin'
A not-remotely-sensationalist display for the 2003 MTV Music Awards.

Lynyrd Skynyrd performing 'Freebird'
The definitive *Old Grey Whistle Test* performance of 1975.

Grace Jones on *Russell Harty*
In 1980, she attacked the utterly inoffensive Russell; the mind boggles as to what she'd do to Jeremy Paxman.

Beyoncé performing 'Crazy in Love'
Two words describe her 2003 *Top of the Pops* performance. 'Ay.' And 'caramba'.

John Lydon on *I'm a Celebrity . . . Get Me Out of Here*
A punk legend. Some emus. Television in 2004 at its most bizarre.

Eleven Beatles References in *The Simpsons*

We all love *The Simpsons* and *The Simpsons* obviously love The Beatles. Here are a mere eleven Fab Four in-jokes.

Marge advises Bart on the theme of peace and love. Homer interrupts, saying, 'Enough of all that Maharishi Gandhi stuff.'

Ringo guest stars. He lives 'somewhere in England' and with the help of a butler named Weatherby is still answering his mid-sixties fan mail.

Lisa's dentist dream sequence turns into a missing scene from the *Yellow Submarine* film: 'Look, it's Lisa in the sky! No diamonds, though.'

In a flashback sequence we see Homer and Moe and others form The Besharps to international Beatlemania-esque fame. They name their second album *Bigger than Jesus*.

Springfield Waxworks contained an exhibit of The Beatles as they appeared on *The Ed Sullivan Show*. Unfortunately, they've melted in a heatwave.

Barney smokes a cigar without removing the wrapper, and sees 'Sgt. Pepper' growing out of Homer's back.

Paul and Linda McCartney guest star. Lisa says, 'I read about you in history class!'

Apu performs 'Sgt. Pepper's Lonely Hearts Club Band' on the tabla.

Apu claims to be 'the fifth Bee-atle'.

Springfield promotes itself as the 'birthplace of The Beatles'.

Ned Flanders has all sorts of Beatles merchandise, including some cans of novelty beverages (John Lemon, Orange Harrison, Paul McIcedTea and Mango Starr). Bart drinks the forty-year-old contents of one can and hallucinates, seeing Milhouse as John Lennon in different stages of his life.

Eleven Great Music Videos

'Video Killed the Radio Star', Buggles once rightly sang – and this was the song that MTV chose to launch with. Here are some of the masters of the art.

'Subterranean Homesick Blues' by Bob Dylan
The forerunner's forerunner. Bob Dylan and D. A. Pennebaker round the back of the Savoy with a load of words on cards. In a word, iconic.

'Bohemian Rhapsody' by Queen
The forerunner. Often said to have invented the video, though thankfully not every video since has contained their four heads spinning round in a circle. In a word, scaramouche.

'Thriller' by Michael Jackson
The Vincent Price is Right of pop videos. Zombies, dancing, that great 'it was just a dream' shot with the red eyes at the end. In two words, scarily good.

'Addicted to Love' by Robert Palmer
The ultimate low-rent video, with a backing band of identikit models for the Yorkshire Bryan Ferry. In a phrase, what's wrong with being sexy?

'Wild Boys' by Duran Duran
Overblown, over-budget, overdone. Still, how often do you get to see Simon Le Bon tied to a windmill and shoved under water? In a word, splash.

'Rock DJ' by Robbie Williams
Similarly, how often does one get to see Robbie Williams ripped to bits? In two words, flesh movie.

'Bittersweet Symphony' by The Verve
Richard Ashcroft walks down the street. That's about it. He does it very well, though. In four words, out of his way.

'Nothing Compares 2 U' by Sinead O'Connor
The track of her tear. Not much compares to this. In a word, heartfelt.

'Cry Me a River' by Justin Timberlake
Justin breaks into the house of someone who looks uncannily like his ex, shags his new girl while 'Britney' is out, then watches 'Miss Spears' take a shower. In a word, creepy.

'Sledgehammer' by Peter Gabriel
The one where the cartoon train goes round his head. In a word, fruity.

'Windowlicker' by Aphex Twin
Voluptuous female bodies, Richard's face grafted on. In a word, freaky.

The Eleven Worst Rock Ideas

When bands stick to their own songs, everything is fine. When they try to stretch out, do something special, tackle another medium, things don't always work out for the best.

The Monkees' appearance in the film *Head*
It was the late 1960s and The Monkees, tired of being the cute TV teen band, all squeaky clean and smiling faces, decided it was time for a change. Enter *Head*, a feature-length concoction of everything psychedelic from drugs to sex, far-outness to non-existent plot-lines. We guess the idea was for The Monkees to be positioned like The Beatles, as a 'proper' band. But they ended up shedding one audience without gaining another. Career suicide, in other words (though a great cult film).

Melanie C's cover of 'Anarchy in the UK'
Following the decision of The Spice Girls to go solo, each Spice had a battle to define themselves as something other than Ginger, Baby, Sporty, Scary or Posh. Mel C, or Melanie C as she was by now calling herself,

eschewed the pop and R&B of her sister spices in favour of a more rock sound. The result was Indie Spice, and an appearance at the V Festival to cement all this newfound credibility. Except that Melanie chose to cover The Pistols' 'Anarchy in the UK', one of rock's great untouchables and particularly not to be touched by un-anarchic pop princesses. It didn't take long for the festival crowd to get the bottles out.

Kevin Rowland's *My Beauty*
Kevin. Kevin, Kevin, Kevin. Stylistically, of course, the whole project was a disaster. Having gone against the grain with various Dexys' wardrobes over the years (the denim gypsy look for *Too Rye Aye*, the American prep look for *Don't Stand Me Down*), Kevin decided to go for the women's-undergarments look for this covers album. For a six-foot bloke with a moustache this was not the most forgiving fashion in which to stage a comeback.

Busted doing 'Teenage Kicks'
Busted, a sort of teenage-friendly Blink-182, are three young boys who have more success than they could ever have dreamt of in their school dormitories, but none of the accompanying cred. 'We're different to all those boy bands,' they implore. 'Look – we can play our instruments.' Which is why, at the Brit Awards 2004 show, they chose to cover what is widely regarded as John Peel's favourite song, 'Teenage Kicks' by The Undertones. On the post-awards TV show, the double-award-winning band asked the editor of *Kerrang!* what he thought of their performance. He summed up the nation's views fairly succinctly.

Madonna's film career
For the love of God, Madonna, no! *Desperately Seeking Susan*, yes, we concede that that was a good idea, but since then Madge's film career has been not so much *Desperately Seeking Susan II* as, well, desperate. The worst moment? *Shanghai Surprise* saw hubby Sean Penn manfully do his marital duty and muck in. But then there was also *Swept Away*, where new hubby Guy Ritchie similarly indulged. In between there was *Who's That Girl?* That girl, of course, being Madonna, because that's the only character she can do.

Janet Jackson's Superbowl performance
The ante for outrageous stunts had been dramatically upped in 2003 by the Britney-Madonna-Christina snogathon at the MTV Awards. It was tacky, but televisually it was just on the right side of respectable. Unlike Janet's performance at the Superbowl half-time show. Justin Timberlake, who emerged from the whole episode surprisingly scot-free, moved on from groping Kylie's bum to exposing Janet's breast. A wardrobe fault was the excuse that no one believed. The result was 200,000 complaints.

Hurricane #1's 'Only the Strongest will Survive' on the *Sun* advert

Hurricane #1 were a later Britpop band in the Oasis mould, who talked the talk and featured former Ride guitarist Andy Bell as songwriter and mainstay. Any credibility they had from being on Creation Records was quickly catapulted out of existence when they agreed to one of their songs being used for a TV campaign for the *Sun*. Blair may have sucked up to Murdoch, but the Indie press were less forgiving and Hurricane #1 saw their status drop from potential new Oasis to pariah overnight. Guess they weren't the strongest.

Prince's contribution to Live Aid

In 1985, Prince was the biggest (and smallest) act on the planet. Purple Rain was reigning everywhere, and when Bob Geldof was getting together the line-up for Live Aid the squiggle who gave great guitar was surely on the wish list. But Prince declined the offer, instead sending a filmed message to be shown to the world – a video of His Purpleness in not very many clothes at all, uttering the words, 'Feed the World'. Strangely, Bob decided not to show this clip.

The twenty-first century Doors

Some bands are, quite simply, inseparable from their front-men. But that doesn't stop some bands from continuing anyway. The Pogues without Shane MacGowan is a disappointing sight, and sound. INXS touring without Michael Hutchence just makes you think, 'Guys, he's *gone*.' But the biggest culprits in our book go to Hutch's inspiration, the original Lizard himself, Jim Morrison. Let's face it, Jim Morrison *is* The Doors. But twenty years in a Parisian grave is not going to stop some tour operators. Enter Ian Astbury from The Cult as stand-in, and a once-great band's legacy grinds miserably into the dust.

Quentin Tarantino's appearance on *American Idol*

The American version of *Pop Idol* that in every way outdoes the British version excelled itself in the 2004 series by allowing one of film's great directors to make himself look like a complete fool. The theme of the week was songs from the cinema, and Quentin, with *Kill Bill Volume Two* to promote, took up the offer of being a guest judge. But, rather than shoot down the out-of-tune competitors with a machine gun full of expletives, Quentin made saccharine judge Paula Abdul look like Simon Cowell in comparison. Did he really compliment one contestant on her version of a Whitney Houston song? The mind, frankly, boggles.

Chris Martin's 'Apple' song

To celebrate the birth of his baby fruit, Chris Martin donned a wig, performed a crap-rap about how Gwyneth wasn't going to 'hump' him for forty-three days, and, er, put it on the Internet for all to see. The joke about having a rush of blood to the head is beneath us.

Eleven Great Rock-Star Appearances on *The Simpsons*

Harry Shearer, who played Derek Smalls in *This is Spinal Tap*, is one of the regular *Simpsons* voices – and, yes, before you mention it, Spinal Tap did feature in their very own *Simpsons* episode. Small world. Thankfully.

And just for completeness here is a list of our eleven favourite rock-star appearances on *The Simpsons*. It must be great being one of their scriptwriters. You think, 'I've always wanted to meet James Brown,' then you write him in the script and next week he's in your studio . . .

Aerosmith do a gig while Moe's is popular. They let Moe sing along on 'Walk this Way'.

Sting takes part in the 'Sending Our Love Down the Well' benefit and the rescue of Bart.

Barry White serves as the grand marshall for Whacking Day. He later helps to save the snakes.

David Crosby helps Lionel Hutz to kick his alcohol addiction.

The Red Hot Chili Peppers guest on *Krusty's Komeback Special*.

The Ramones heckle Burns at his birthday party.

James Brown sings at the 'Do What You Feel' Festival.

Peter Frampton gets the short end of the stick: Homer ruins his pig, Cypress Hill steal his orchestra, and Sonic Youth steal his watermelon.

The Smashing Pumpkins advise Homer on being a super-freak.

The boys from U2 help Homer to win his campaign against the sanitation engineer voiced by Steve Martin.

Dolly Parton springs Homer and his pals from jail.

FILTHY LUCRE

Eleven Nuggets of Financial Wisdom from the Rock Elite

Sting
'When you're as rich as I am, you don't have to be political.'

Madonna
'I like to show off when I'm on stage, but I don't like to show off, like, "Come in and check it out. Look how rich I am." That's not my style.'

Boy George
'With the punk thing, everyone was making impractical attacks on being rich or having money, ya know, but they all wanted to be rich.'

Cher
'I'm scared to death of being poor. It's like a fat girl who loses 500 pounds but is always fat inside. I grew up poor and will always feel poor inside. It's my pet paranoia.'

Brad Whifford (Aerosmith)
'We owe each other a lot of money. Touring is the only way we'll ever pay each other back.'

Courtney Love
'It's incredibly easy not to be a musician. It's always a struggle and a dangerous career choice. We are motivated by passion and by money.'

Elvis Presley
'It's not how much you have that makes people look up to you, it's who you are.'

David Lee Roth
'Money can't buy you happiness, but it can buy you a yacht big enough to pull up right beside it.'

Garth Brooks
'You aren't wealthy until you have something money can't buy.'

Elvis Presley (again)
'Sharing money is what gives it its value.'

Mick Jagger
'We've always done it for the money.'

Eleven Items of Rock Memorabilia We Would Like to Own

Attics all over the world are being cleared and torrents of rock memorabilia are pouring on to the market – whether through the regular Sotheby's auctions or the twenty-four/seven world of eBay. If you ever wanted to buy a piece of history (no matter how obscure) then now is your chance.

The 'Candle in the Wind' lyric sheet
Specifically, Bernie Taupin's handwritten lyrics for the version of his song sung by Elton John at the funeral of Diana, Princess of Wales. They were sold in February 1998 for just under $500,000. This works out at approximately $300 per gut-wrenching second – what a bargain.

John Lennon's Gallotone 'Champion' acoustic guitar
As sold by Sotheby's in September 1999 for £155,500. The guitar was played by Lennon with his group The Quarrymen at a church fête on 6 July 1957 – the day he first met Paul McCartney.

The stage on which John met Paul
Fancy paying over the odds for a few planks of wood, a bag of screws and some badly written assembly instructions? Instead of going to IKEA you could bid for the stage from St Peter's Church Hall, Woolton, Merseyside, where John met Paul at the aforementioned church fête. It was recently withdrawn from auction at Bill Wyman's Sticky Fingers restaurant when it failed to reach its reserve price, so you might get a bargain.

An autographed, full-size electric Kramer focus
This could be yours, for between $7,000 and $10,000. It features forty-four signatures, including those of Jon Bon Jovi, Gene Simmons, Sheryl Crow, Eric Clapton and Bruce Springsteen.

The glasses Buddy Holly died in

Visibly scarred, these heavy black-rimmed specs were discovered in 1994 in an Iowa sheriff's-office desk drawer, where they'd been for twenty-two years. In 1998, they were sold at auction by Holly's widow, Maria Elena, for $80,000 and ended up in the Buddy Holly exhibit in Lubbock. You wouldn't be able to resist trying them on and crooning, 'That'll be the day . . .' would you?

Justin Timberlake's breakfast

In a 2002 eBay auction, student Kathy Summers paid $1,025 for a half-eaten piece of Justin's French toast. New York radio station WHTZ/Z100 FM had put the item up for bid as a joke, after Timberlake had appeared on a morning show, and it came complete with his plastic fork, plate and napkin. The station matched the sum paid by Ms Summers and the whole lot went to charity.

John Lennon's piano

The 1970 piano on which he wrote 'Imagine' was bought at auction in 2002 for £1.45m by George Michael. Rumour has it that he outbid Noel Gallagher and Robbie Williams.

Keith Moon's drum kit

At Sotheby's in 1991, a mere £16,000 could have bought you a portion of Who drummer Keith Moon's Premier Part-Drum Kit, *circa* 1968. This stunning lot, in chrome finish, comprised a 22-in bass drum with group logo on the front skin; two 16-in floor tom-toms; two 14-in hanging tom-toms; two bass-drum spurs; and one tom-tom post. Slight chlorine damage.

Michael Jackson's white glove

Who wouldn't want to wear such a potent symbol of Jackson at his career peak? As seen on *that* video and *that* album cover? An original trademark glove, as worn during the *Thriller* era and featuring 'solid-application, off-white iridescent sequins', was sold on eBay in August 2004 for a cool $5,500. Just think what it would have gone for had they removed the 'Made in Hong Kong' label – and if he ever finds the other one to complete the pair, well . . .

Jimi Hendrix's amp

At Kathy Etchinham's Drugscope charity auction in June 2001, her late boyfriend's Marshall super amplifier, estimated value £8,000 to £12,000, went to an anonymous bidder for £33,350. Imagine what we'd have paid for it if it had gone up to eleven. The mind boggles.

Johnny Rotten's T-shirt
His Westwood/McLaren-designed 'Anarchy' shirt was sold at auction in London in 2001 for £3,995. Dry-clean only – some stains may not come out.

Eleven Corporate Whores and Sponsored Tours

If it moves, slap a logo on it – but does this have the desired effect on the fans? Do they make the leap and give the sponsors a good return on their investment?

Would you see The Goo Goo Dolls and rush off to buy a car?
In 2002, General Motors made their first foray into music sponsorship with The Goo Goo Dolls' summer tour. Jill Lajdziak, vice-president of Saturn sales, service and marketing. 'The new Saturn ION line allows self-expression, so music was a natural association for the product. The tour will help generate awareness among younger buyers that Saturn has designed a product for them.' Verdict: Sorry? What? Who? Why?

Could Ozzy convince you to buy a PS2?
'Ozzfest is a great opportunity for Sony Computer Entertainment America to bring the PlayStation 2 experience straight to our gamers who are also metal fans, many of whom attend the festival year after year,' apparently. Grand prize-winners will also receive a PlayStation 2 computer entertainment system autographed by Ozzy himself. Verdict: Ozztastic.

Would ZZ Top make you reach for a Miller Lite?
Disaster almost struck on a recent ZZ Top tour when their support act The Black Crowes repeatedly insulted the tour sponsor, Miller Beer, on stage. The solution? Go crack open a beer or two and sort it out? Er, no – ZZ Top sacked The Black Crowes instead. Verdict: Good thinking, hairy blokes.

Would Kylie live make you want to get into her pants?
Kylie's managers just couldn't get the thought of sponsorship out of their heads and for her 2002 tour signed sponsorship deals for almost every part of her body – from Kylie wearing Dolce et Gabbana on stage to bottles of special 'Kylie'-labelled Evian water on sale and her dancers wearing Agent Provocateur underwear. More recently she has launched

the Love Kylie lingerie range, including the 'Lucky Knickers' which 'come with Kylie's seal of approval'. Verdict: Blimey! We should be so lucky.

Would The Rolling Stones in concert make you think of buying perfume?

In 1981, die-hard rock fans felt rather emasculated by the news that The Rolling Stones had signed the perfume manufacturer JOVAN as main sponsor for their Wheels of Steel world tour. Verdict: Seeing Jagger sweating buckets as he runs miles traversing the arena stage, your mind doesn't immediately turn to beautiful aromas and subtle olfactory delights, does it?

Would seeing Courtney's Hole make you rush for a soft drink?

Courtney Love said that her corporate partners treated her like 'an ungrateful little bitch who should be grovelling for the experience to play for their damn soda', but, being Courtney, she didn't take it lying down – oh no. She played topless and drank rival cola onstage. *You go, girl!* She said that in future the only product she'd consider accepting sponsorship from is sanitary towels. Verdict: What a bloody mess.

Beverley Craven

Sorry, Courtney, but Bev got there first with Tampax. Verdict: Only works at certain times of the month.

Would Britney make you switch on MTV?

MTV decided to roll out its first global-tour sponsorship with the MTV Presents Britney Spears Onyx Hotel World Tour 2004. Shame that the tour got dreadful reviews, and that Britney was accused of miming, had her fifty-five-hour marriage dissolved and then injured herself causing multiple dates to be cancelled. Oh well – more time to watch MTV, we suppose. Verdict: Oops.

Marvel at Justin's six-pack and buy a Big Mac? Iffy, we should say!

The subtly named 'McDonald's Presents Justin Timberlake Justified World Tour and Lovin' It Live' tour even had a promotional McSong, entitled surprisingly, 'I'm Lovin' It', which reached the Top Ten in the US. Actually Justin would probably have done it for free: 'I love what McDonald's is doing with this new campaign and it's cool to be part of it.' Verdict: Trying a bit too hard.

Watch the King of Pop and drink the King of Pops? Maybe . . .

Michael Jackson negotiated a cool $10,000,000 sponsorship package with Pepsi for his 1981 Bad world tour, but all we can remember about it was that his hair caught fire during the filming of an advert. Verdict: Shame.

See The Stones and reach for your mobile? You're learning fast, boys!
For their Forty Licks tour they linked up with T-Mobile, but they also struck
a side deal with Future Forests and CarbonNeutral Touring for the tour's
UK leg whereby for every fifty-seven fans who drove to a Stones gig it was
guaranteed that one tree would be planted to offset the emissions from their
vehicles. The UK now has 280 new trees as a result. Verdict: Next time you
have a huge pile of leaves blocking an outside drain or sticking to your
windscreen, just call Mick or Keith from your mobile and they'll be right
over. Once they start to pick them up they will probably never ever stop.

If you run a huge multinational and would like to give us some free money
for putting your name on the cover of future *Elevens* volumes then please
email juanlauda@rockandpopelevens.com. The more inappropriate the
link-up, the better.

I Fought the Law and the Law Won (Sometimes): Eleven Cases where Rock went Legal

Tony McCarroll versus Oasis
The original Oasis drummer sued his former bandmates for a massive £16
million in 1999, claiming unfair dismissal. He settled for a paltry (and
taxable) £550,000, out of which he had to pay an estimated £250,000 in
costs. When one considers that in 2002 Oasis received a heart-stopping
amount of money to use 'Live Forever' in a car commercial, you realize
that McCarroll should probably not have cracked open the champagne
supernova and may still have reason to look back in anger.

Robbie Williams versus the Woody Guthrie estate
In 2002 a High Court judge ruled that Robbie Williams did not have to
pay damages for copying lyrics from a 1961 Woody Guthrie song but that
he must pay 25 per cent of the income from his album track 'Jesus in a
Camper Van', which by now amounts to about £50,000. 'Jesus in a
Camper Van' contains lyrics that a judge had previously decided were
'substantially' copied from a song by Loudon Wainwright III, which in
turn was based on 'I am the Way' by late folk singer Guthrie. The
copyright holders had tried to claim up to 100 per cent of the income of
the Williams track, which is owned by more than 2.5 million people in the
UK on the album *I've Been Expecting You*, but Mr Justice Pumphrey said
that additional damages were not justified because the copyright

infringement was not cynical or flagrant and the song had no particular 'staying power'. Unlike Robbie, obviously.

Van Morrison versus Gary Marlow
In 2003 a British court ordered veteran rock star Van Morrison to pay £40,000 in damages to the owner of the Crown Hotel in Everligh, Wiltshire. Gary Marlow had sued the fifty-eight-year-old singer and his production company, Exile, for up to £400,000 for the cancellation of a concert at the hotel, but Justice Peter Creswell ruled that Marlow was entitled to only £40,000, including a £20,000 advance fee paid to Exile. In a written ruling the judge voiced his 'considerable concerns' about Mr Marlow's evidence to substantiate the claim, which he thought 'excessive'. And Morrison's reason for pulling out? He said that Marlow was in breach of the agreement not to publicize the concert.

Roger Waters versus Pink Floyd
At the end of 1985, Roger Waters left Pink Floyd. Instead of writing them a nice Wish You Were Here thank-you card, he immediately sued the remaining band members for exclusive rights to all the works of Pink Floyd, including the name. The legal battle lasted over a year but was settled out of court when Dave Gilmour brokered a deal whereby Waters would receive rights to *The Wall* and royalties for works he contributed to.

Mattel versus Aqua
Do you remember that infectious summer hit of 1997 'Barbie Girl' by the popular beat combo Aqua? The lyrics were far from innocuous and Mattel, the begetters of Barbie dolls, sued Aqua and their record company, MCA, for unspecified damages for associating their huge-breasted plastic toy with 'sexual and other unsavoury themes', 'trademark violation', false description and unfair competition. Obviously the case was dismissed, but don't feel too sorry for Mattel – placed head to toe, Barbie dolls and their friends sold since 1959 would circle the earth more than seven times and in the time it has taken you to read this paragraph another twenty have been sold.

Anonymous versus Tupac Shakur
In November 1996 a woman brought a $16.6 million lawsuit against the murdered rap star Tupac Shakur's estate after she was paralyzed from being shot in the back at a 1993 Tupac concert in an Arkansas nightclub. The ruling was later overturned but she did trouser $2 million in damages.

Numerous versus Dr Dre
What is it with mild-mannered Dr Dre? Court papers in an ongoing $10 million copyright dispute brought by a French jazz composer state that Dre also had to pay $1.5 million to London's Minder Music Ltd for lifting

a bass line for his *Chronic 2001* album's 'Let's Get High' in 2003. Apparently the LA producer also had to cough up galactic amounts of money for using the THX sonic-boom sound *Star Wars* creator George Lucas uses in movies. Apparently Dre was warned not to use the sound on his 1999 multi-platinum *Chronic 2001*, but used it anyway.

Blue versus Blue
In 2003 boy-band Blue settled a High Court battle with an old-man band of rockers also called Blue who had had a number-eighteen hit in 1977 with 'Gonna Capture Your Heart' and thought the public might get confused as to which Blue was which. After no doubt asking what 'pop music' was, a judge pointed out that the two bands were unlikely to be confused, notably because of the age difference. The little-boy Blues and EMI/Virgin were awarded £100,000 costs, which they agreed not to collect on condition that the seventies rockers made no further claims against them. Who's blue now, then?

Samuel Bourdin versus Madonna
On the eve of the launch of the Reinvention tour, Madonna settled a copyright-infringement lawsuit regarding her 'Hollywood' video, brought by the son of the acclaimed French photographer Guy Bourdin. Bourdin's son Samuel claimed that her video was a rip-off of his father's erotic images. 'It's one thing to draw inspiration; it's quite another to simply plagiarize the heart and soul of my father's work,' Bourdin said at the time. Madonna acknowledged no wrongdoing but Bourdin's lawyer, John Koegel, said the parties reached a 'very, very successful settlement'.

Gus Dudgeon versus David Bowie
In 2002 David Bowie was sued for £1 million by producer Gus Dudgeon, who worked on his 1969 classic single 'Space Oddity' but claims he got paid only £250. Dudgeon sought a one-off payment of £1 million or a cut of earnings, plus interest and damages stretching back over the past thirty years to when the song was first recorded. Also in that year Dudgeon sued Universal's This Record Company over unpaid royalties from fourteen Elton John albums. Tragically he died in a car crash before either of these cases reached a conclusion. Ashes to ashes?

Jason Alexander versus Britney Spears?
As this book went to press we were still waiting to see whether Britney's husband of fifty-five hours, Jason Alexander, was going to take her to court for a cut of the profits from her Toxic tour – even though their brief marriage ended months before she hit the road. A friend says, 'He's really trying to stick it to her.' Too late now, one imagines. He had a whole fifty-five hours to get that right.

The Eleven Steps from Hero to Zero

Picture the scene: you have a steady job and play with a band at the weekends. You are spotted by an A&R man from a big label and your dreams come true – they want to sign you. And what's more, they offer you and your three bandmates half a million pounds between you.

Step one
Champagne all round and news stories appear about 'Local Band Signs Six-Figure Recording Contract'. You give up your job. Colleagues ask you to remember them when you're famous.

Step two
You begin to realize that this half-million is less a pay-cheque and more a budget. You book a rehearsal room and studio time, and hire session musicians, a producer and an engineer. You cut your first album. All this costs you £250,000, leaving you with £250,000.

Step three
You pay twenty per cent commission to your manager, leaving you with £200,000.

Step four
You pay £25,000 each to your lawyer and business-affairs manager, leaving you with £150,000.

Step five
You pay £70,000 in taxes, leaving £80,000 to split between the four of you in the band. You now have £20,000 each to live off for eighteen months until the record is released. You start to practise saying, 'Do you want fries with that?' just in case.

Step six
The record comes out and amazingly sells half a million copies so you release two singles and make two videos.

Step seven
The videos cost your record company half a million pounds and is 100 per cent recoupable out of your royalties. Basically you have spent all of your half a million already and are beginning to spend money you don't have.

Step eight
The record company spends a further £150,000 on essential independent radio promotion which is, you've guessed it, 100 per cent recoupable

against royalties, as is the original half-million-pound advance. You now 'owe' the record company £1,150,000, which you must earn back before you'll see another penny.

Step nine
In the unlikely event that all the half-million records are sold at full price you will 'earn' £2 a record – a grand total of £1,000,000. But . . .

Step ten
Your £1,000,000 royalty income less the recoupable £1,150,000 means you have had a platinum debut album and devoted two years of your life for £20,000 each and you still owe the record company £150,000.

Step eleven
You fire your manager. Your new manager looks at your royalty statement and cheers you up by explaining that the record company have grossed £5,500,000 and made a profit of about £3,250,000. Then he looks at your contract and discovers that you have signed away your copyright for life.

Start again.

Eleven of the Highest-Grossing Tours of All Time

Next time you buy your £50 concert ticket, £15 CD, £20 tour brochure and £18 T-shirt, just stop to think where all this money's going . . .

The Rolling Stones, Voodoo Lounge (1994/1995): $320 million
Their Forty Licks tour grossed a piss-poor $299.5 million. Maybe they needed additional snooker balls on that one?

U2, Elevation (2001): $175 million
Less the cost of international phone calls?

Bruce Springsteen, tour with The E Street Band (1993): $181.7 million
Less the costs of stars and stripes?

Michael Jackson, Bad (1987/1988): $125 million
Not bad at all.

Pink Floyd, Division Bell (1994): $103,500,000
Mondeo-driving Jeremy Clarkson clones filled the stadiums.

*NSync, PopOdyssey (2001): $86 million
Just-in time, really. That ain't going to happen again.

Celine Dion, Las Vegas residency (2002): $80.5 million
Less the cost of room service?

Cher, Farewell (1993): $76.3 million
Less the cost of cryonic suspension tanks backstage?

Fleetwood Mac, Say What You Will (2003/2004): $69.2 million
Less the cost of hiring roadies to blow class-As up some of their fundaments through straws? Just rumours, we are sure.

The Eagles, Hell Freezes Over (1994): $67.5 million
Less hotel costs?

Paul McCartney, Driving USA (2002): $103.3 million
With a set including loads of Beatles classics, you can't go wrong.

Eleven Unusual Charitable Donations

Singing on a charity record is one thing, but we really admire the stars who thought laterally . . .

Mick Jagger
In November 2000, Sotheby's auctioned embroidery by some of Britain's most dangerous criminals on behalf of the charity Fine Cell Work, an organization dedicated to teaching embroidery and quilt-making in prison. One of the designs they worked on was by The Stones' most famous seamstress.

Madonna
In August 2001, a sale of memorabilia donated by Madge raised over $200,000 for charity to tie in with the launch of her Reality tour. A mere $23,850 would have bought you one of her beaded Dolce et Gabbana bras; for the less bedroom-minded, the handwritten lyrics for 'Like a Prayer' went for $20,000.

Hugh Grant

Grant paid £200,000 at Elton John's AIDS Foundation's 2003 White Tie and Tiara Ball to have dinner with one of his best friends – er, Elton John. We hope Elton did the washing-up.

Bono

Bono was one of fifty-two Irish celebrities who designed and signed their own playing card to raise money at an auction for Dublin-based charity the Irish Hospice Foundation, which provides care and services for the terminally ill. Bono's Mephisto-like drawing of himself as the joker went for a pleasing £3,500.

Boy George

In January 2004, Boy George donated the handwritten lyrics for 'Karma Chameleon' to his friend Laura Gosein to help her raise sponsorship for Trek Peru, a fundraising challenge she was undertaking for Leonard Cheshire Homes. She raised £700 by selling the lyrics on eBay.

Paul McCartney

US businessman Ralph Whitworth decided to give his wife Wendy a present of Macca for her birthday. Sir Paul accepted a fee of $1 million for his charity, Adopt-A-Minefield, and delivered a blistering ninety-minute surprise set, including several Beatles numbers, to the Whitworths and their 150 guests. For the finale Wendy was invited on stage to dance with him. Fab!

Celine Dion

In March 2002, Dion was presented with the most expensive disc ever made in recognition of her 15 million album and single sales in the UK and immediately donated it to the Capital FM Help a London Child annual charity auction. The one-of-a-kind diamond-encrusted silver disc was designed and manufactured by the Queen's jewellers, Asprey & Garrard. It raised £70,000.

Eric Clapton

Eric sold fifty-six guitars at auction on 24 June 2004, to raise money for the drug-rehabilitation clinic the Crossroads Centre located in Antigua. His prized Stratocaster 'Blackie' was sold for $959,500, becoming the most expensive guitar ever to have been sold at auction, and a new world record was set for the sale of a Gibson guitar: Clapton's 1964 red Gibson ES-335 brought $847,500.

Sting

At an April 2002 New York auction to raise money for his rainforest charity, people were given the chance to win a unique opportunity: Sting recording the outgoing ansafone message for the highest bid. When the bidding only reached $30,000 Sting leapt into the middle of the dining room and performed a striptease, which ended with the removal of his shirt, a lot of applause and a winning bid of $100,000.

Mariah Carey

The diva gave some interesting items for an online fundraising auction for the Knowledge is Power (KIP) Foundation. She offered a butterfly-studded bra, which raised $1,000, and a pair of her boxer shorts inscribed with the tasteful message 'I used to sleep in these – among other things of that nature.' Classy.

Macy Gray

Celebrities were asked to be photographed wearing a pair of Jimmy Choos for the Elton John AIDS Foundation, but singer Macy Gray took things one step further. The lights came up for the encore at a 2004 London gig to find Macy sitting astride a chair, naked bar a pair of Jimmy Choos. Did she stumble when she tried to walk away?

Eleven of Rock's Richest

According to 2003's The *Sunday Times* Rich List, the Top Eleven richest people in the music industry were the following:

Clive Calder (£1,235 billion)

Who? Good question. He was a talent scout for EMI and then founded Zomba Records, which developed a list of talent that included Britney, The Backstreet Boys and *NSync. In 2002, BMG bought Zomba for a cool £1.235 billion. If you put £1.235 billion in the bank at five per cent interest, you'd receive £62m million a year.

Sir Paul McCartney (£760 million)

He wrote the songs that made the whole world sing. The Beatles are still the best-selling group ever – in 2002, their *1* compilation sold almost 14 million copies in the first month of release. A Beatles song is always playing somewhere in the world.

Simon Fuller (£220 million)

The man who brought the world The Spice Girls and *Pop Idol*. Well, none out of two ain't bad.

Madonna (and Guy) (£215 million)
Obviously much of this worth comes from their massively successful movie *Swept Away*, but we suppose the music must contribute a small amount towards the total.

Robert Stigwood (£200 million)
Stigwood is a heavy-hitting rock impresario/svengali/promoter. You may only just have heard the name, but, if we say *Grease, Saturday Night Fever*, The Bee Gees, Bowie, Clapton, *Evita*, you'll get the picture.

Sir Mick Jagger (£180 million)
After child-support and contraception there is obviously still a lot of money left.

Sir Elton John (£175 million)
Love him or loathe him, we all know all the songs and, if we are being honest, have one of the CDs (or a 7-inch single of him duetting with Kiki Dee on 'Don't Go Breaking My Heart').

Sting (£175 million)
That high-rise development he is planning in the Amazon rainforest will boost his net worth even more next year. Not.

Keith Richards (£165 million)
Just think how much higher up the charts he would be if he hadn't spent so much on 'substances'?

Tom Jones (£165 million)
Not many people know this, but Tom Jones employs a member of staff to collect the knickers strewn across the stage at the end of his performances. They are then dry-cleaned, repackaged and sold on to some very well-known high-street stores. Nowadays most of his income comes from this venture, not from spending forty years in the musical aristocracy. If only.

Phil Collins (£130 million)
One almost feels sorry for little Phil down here at the bottom of the list. What does a mere £130 million buy you these days?

Eleven Very Tasteful Pieces of Rock Merchandise

These days, rock stars can't rely on record sales alone to fund their bling-bling lifestyle. You can see how tempting it is to license your image – but, while some people do it with style, others get it horribly wrong, putting their names to what we could politely call 'tat' and impolitely call 'real tat'.

If you could choose only one of the following, which one would it be?

Ozzy Osbourne's heavy pewter ring
(Now *there*'s an image to conjure with.) The rings feature a '3-D logo cut deep into the metal', apparently. And they are officially licensed and approved by Ozzy himself! Each design is 'reviewed personally by the band members for approval so you know these designs are sweet'. $10.95

Celine Dion's 'A New Day has Come' leather coaster set
This is so you can 'be ready when guests show up at home or the office'. Each set of four matte black leather, cork-backed coasters features Celine's signature logo and 'A New Day has Come' embossed in gold, and comes in a keepsake box. $25.

Metallica's pint glass
Each one features a Metallica embossed logo on the side and 'a hidden black scary guy on the bottom'. $9.

Billy Joel's bobble-head doll
Apparently 'a classic collector's item'. The figure stands 6 inches tall, with Billy's trademark black suit painted on, and shows him holding a microphone in his left hand. $14.95.

The Kiss KISS-opoly game
This game allows players to trade their gold records for platinum records, and gets them wondering if they'll be 'Hired as a roadie to set up the Catman's drums' or if they 'Win 2nd Place in the Girls of KISS Beauty Contest!' $24.95.

Britney Spears' rhinestone onyx girls' camisole
Black 100 per cent cotton girls' camisole featuring 'ONYX' on the front set in a rhinestone appliqué; the circle Britney logo is printed on the upper back. $17.95.

Rod Stewart's 'Tonight's the night' panties
Black – not tartan, sadly – cotton knickers with 'Tonight's the Night' printed on the front. $12.95.

The Dixie Chicks' 'Blinky Light'
This you can use 'as an earring, a button or cufflink' so you can 'flash the world that you are a Chicks fan'. Normal price $15 but now an incredible $4.98. Going fast, we imagine.

Michael Jackson's 'HIStory' coin card
Featuring the 'HIStory' collectible Michael Jackson coins. A HYSterical $54.95.

Fleetwood Mac's stuffed-toy penguin
It'll be wearing a miniature black-and-white T-shirt with the Fleetwood Mac 'FM' logo on it (as worn by Stevie Nicks?). $14.95.

Madonna's hand-signed rhinestone portrait
An 'extraordinary appliqué of true crystal rhinestones and metal nailheads, this incredible piece is on ultrasuede, hand-signed and framed'. $1,500.

Be honest – you want them all, don't you?

Eleven Ways to Blow Your Wad

OK: you're a huge star, but what do you do with all your cash? As a service to those rock stars out there who are kicking their heels and in need of some retail therapy, we are proud to present a handy guide to spending all that money, money, money . . .

Eat take-aways
On 1 February 1976, Elvis called the Colorado Mine Company restaurant in Denver, ordered a take-out of 22 Fool's Gold Loaves (a 42,000-calorie sandwich-for-one made in a hollowed-out loaf of bread filled with one large jar each of grape jelly and peanut butter plus a pound of bacon) and flew the 1,000-mile four-hour round trip to collect his order. He should have got them to deliver.

Spoil your kids rotten
Ex-Spice Girl (remember them?) Victoria Beckham (remember her?) spent

a reported £20,000 creating a domed roof complete with glow-in-the-dark stars for her son Brooklyn's bedroom in her and David's 'Beckingham Palace' home. The room also features a mural of Posh as Cinderella and Becks as Prince Charming. Classy.

Like pretty flowers
According to evidence given in a London court case, Elton John once spent £30 million in just two years – which included a massive £293,000 on flowers. When quizzed about this he said simply, 'Yes, I like flowers.' Luckily he didn't like chrysanthemums, because the cost would have spiralled . . .

Acquire an expensive wife
Lionel Richie's ex-wife Diane said that as a couple they regularly spent more than $300,000 a month and that she had free rein to spend 'as much money as I wanted on whatever I chose'. Her *monthly* expenses included $15,000 for clothing/shoes/accessories, $600 *each* on Pilates, massages and therapy and $250 on sharpening her nails.

Divorce her
Rod Stewart once said, 'Instead of getting married again, I'm going to find a woman I don't like and just give her a house.'

Keep very clean
Madonna's LA home has all the usual trappings of success – sauna, pool, gym, screening room and seven bedrooms. But curiously sports *fifteen* bathrooms. We know she's filthy rich, but that is ridiculous.

Put a fish in your tank
Rap star Wyclef Jean installed a huge fish tank in the boot of his Hummer car. In it he has a 4-ft(ish)-long shark. When asked why he said, 'You know, all people open their trunks and there's a huge sound system in there . . . but I wanted to surprise people, and I wanted to hear the sounds of the ocean instead.'

Build your own private world and divorce yourself from reality
Michael Jackson, the self-styled Peter Pan of Pop, took his obsession with the J. M. Barrie story one step further and built a huge theme park and zoo in the grounds of his 2,600-acre fantasy world Neverland in the Santa Ynez Valley.

Wear women's stuff but in a macho kind of way
Clearly you have to be incredibly macho to get away with wearing full-length pure white mink coats, carrying diamond-topped canes and

wearing sparkling jewellery worth more than most people's houses. Or, like Puff Daddy/P. Diddy, you just have to be so rich that no one will call you a big wuss to your face.

Get yourself a good haircut
The scissors that cut Britney Spears' hair allegedly cost $3,000 and are especially imported from Japan. Wouldn't it be cheaper to fly to Tokyo and get her hair cut there?

Be irrational and take drugs
In court Elton John failed to recall an occasion in Easter 1990 when he had arranged for accountants to be flown out to the US to discuss 'a serious financial crisis' but had then refused to meet them when they arrived. The only explanation he could give to the court was that prior to July 1990, when he overcame his addiction, he was 'a serious cocaine addict' suffering from irrational moods. As Aerosmith's Steve Tyler once said, 'I heard that your brain stops growing when you start doing drugs. Let's see, I guess that makes me nineteen.'

Eleven Rock Stars who Have Two Jobs to Help Pay the Rent

It's hard enough to get one successful career going these days, but the following rock stars manage at least two. You could say that they are wisely diversifying in preparation for the time when they can no longer fit into the leather trousers and the back catalogue starts to slacken off. Or, if you were to be totally cynical, you could say that they are able to play at being anything they want . . .

Bill Wyman
His highly successful and recently relaunched Sticky Fingers restaurant in Kensington, London, has been going strong since 1989 – four years before he quit as bassist for The Rolling Stones. Check out the rock 'n' roll memorabilia on display and, who knows, he could be waiting at your table or just hanging around in the background looking moody. He's good at that.

Beyoncé
In the 'hair today, gone tomorrow' world of entertainment, one celebrity has her head properly screwed on. Not content with being a bootylicious

platinum-selling singer and actress, Beyoncé Knowles also, according to MTV.com, earns some $4 million for just ten days' work a year advertising hair products. This should see her through any bad times destiny might throw her way.

Roger Daltrey
Maybe he actually shouted 'Hope I fry before I get old' on 'My Generation' – besides those infamous green-wellies ads for American Express, his diverse business interests include the running of a lucrative fish farm in Inverness. There you go, sir – cod and chips twice. Now, who's next?

Dolly Parton
There's the Dollywood theme park – 'more musical live entertainment than any other theme park in America' – the obligatory Dolly Parton Museum and such irresistible delights as the Southern Gospel Music Hall of Fame and Museum, but forget all that. The main attraction has to be Doggywood™, which is 'a one-of-a-kind, climate-controlled indoor dog-care facility'. Enough already.

Bob Geldof
Sir Bob has never been someone to let the grass grow under his feet. Post-Live Aid, he diversified in setting up one of Europe's most successful independent production companies, Planet 24, which is best known for producing programmes such as *The Big Breakfast, The Word, Survivor* and, er, *Watercolour Challenge*. In recent years alone, he released a new album, started touring again and set up a new production company.

Peter Gabriel
In 1982, he set up the international festival of world music and dance, WOMAD, which is now one of the UK's flagship music events. He also achieved every rock star's dream by building his own recording studio, Real World. Many other such projects have failed, but time at Real World is always booked years ahead, the studio being among Europe's most innovative and technologically advanced. Not a sign of an egg box glued to the wall, then?

Sean Combs
The artist otherwise known as Puff Daddy/P. Diddy founded and still runs the highly successful Bad Boy Worldwide Entertainment Group, which now has a $300 million annual turnover and encompasses everything from artist management to restaurants, music publishing to clothing. How he has time to do all this and change his name regularly is quite beyond us, but he appears to manage it very successfully.

Ronnie Wood
When he isn't busy being one of the world's best (and busiest) guitarists, Wood turns his hand to painting – pictures depicting some of the rock 'n' roll greats he has played alongside as well as some work of a slightly more esoteric nature. He has made more than $3 million from his art to date and its popularity has nothing to do with his day job. Not.

Boy George
Having crafted a busy second life for himself as a club DJ, he ploughs the club circuit internationally as well as playing lucrative events for clients such as Versace. He also has a small fashion line, making (himself) shirts, T-shirts and trousers which are soon to be mass-produced for Harvey Nicks.

Snoop Dogg
The rapper teamed up with *Hustler*'s Larry Flynt to release *Doggystyle*, which is basically a hardcore porn movie with a few songs thrown into the mix. Although Dogg doesn't appear in the, erm, 'non-music' sections, his fingerprints are all over the film. Well, at least the fingerprints of one hand. Nice work if you can get it.

Dave Stewart
In partnership with Microsoft's Paul G. Allen, this is another rock star doin' it for himself. The Eurythmics star opened the mega-exclusive 'entertainment and leisure complex' The Hospital in London's Covent Garden. It includes television, recording and dubbing studios, a screening room, facilities for film post-production, a public restaurant, gallery and café and a private members' club. Sweet dreams, indeed . . .

Ker-ching!

INTO THE GROOVE

Eleven Great Songs that Only Got to Number Eleven

What more can we say? Poetry in numbers.

'Shakermaker' by Oasis

'Panic' by The Smiths

'Coffee & TV' by Blur

'Undercover of the Night' by The Rolling Stones

'Sorry Seems to be the Hardest Word' by Elton John

'Love Me Tender' by Elvis Presley

'Pleasant Valley Sunday' by The Monkees

'Opportunities (Let's Make Lots of Money)' by The Pet Shop Boys

'Girls and Boys' by Prince

'London Calling' by The Clash

'Suicide Blonde' by INXS

The Eleven Worst-Ever Charity Records

Charity – or *charidee*, to give it its proper pronunciation – may be borne of the loftiest of intentions, but the end product is not always given generously. With these examples below, it would have been better to give the money spent on the single straight to charity and avoid buying a record that you knew you'd never play . . .

'We are the World' by various artists
Band Aid was a great idea and, of its type, a half-decent song. 'We are the World' Disneyfied it. Gone were the punchy, hard-hitting lyrics and in came mawkish rubbish about being the 'children'. Lowlight was the 'duet' between Bruce Springsteen and Michael Jackson, in which they respectively growled and squeaked the first two lines of the chorus.

'Band Aid II' by various artists
Band Aid was a great idea and, of its type, a half-decent song. 'Band Aid II' Stock, Aitken and Watermanned it. Goodbye, Bono, Sting and Boy George. Hello, Jason Donovan, Big Fun and Bros. This second version is not often found on those *Best Christmas Albums in the World . . . Ever!* albums. Funny, that.

'The Stonk' by Hale and Pace
Not so much the stonk as the stinker of the various Comic Relief singles that have come out over the years. With Hale and Pace doing the honours, it must have been a quiet year. 'The Stonk' was a form of dance that was almost rude, almost funny, but not quite.

'It Takes Two' by Bruno and Liz
However bad Hale and Pace were, they were Morecambe and Wise to Bruno Brookes and Liz Kershaw, who were, you'll recall, eighties weekend DJs with a hilarious routine of pretending to hate each other. We think they argued through this Children in Need single as well, though we can't quite remember, having erased its contents for the sanity of our minds.

'Candle in the Wind' by Elton John
Goodbye, Norma Jean as Bernie Taupin's hastily scribbled Diana rewrite swapped Hollywood icon for English rose. We have two problems: firstly, the new lyrics didn't actually scan; and secondly, people tried to show how much they loved Diana by buying the single by the dozen. In any other week, such block-buying would be seen as rigging the chart and the record would be banned. Instead, of course, the single stayed at number one for ever.

'Sgt. Pepper Knew my Father' by various artists
Twenty years on from *Sgt. Pepper*, the *NME* decided that it would be a great idea to get the top bands of the day (plus Wet Wet Wet) to re-record

the album song by song, all in aid of Childline. The cover features a picture of a train (no, we're not sure why either), but really a car crash might have been a better idea. If you want to hear The Fall 'play' 'A Day in the Life', this is the album for you.

'Perfect Day' by various artists
Was it just us, or did everyone miss the point? The original Lou Reed song, as correctly used in *Trainspotting*, is about the joys of heroin. Quite what it is doing in this Children in Need advert for all things BBC, God only knows. And as for whoever it is who sings 'Reap! Reap!' like some sort of soul chick at the end, well, put it this way: we don't think it 'perfect'.

'Band Aid III' by various artists
Thankfully never more than a pipe dream. The plan was to get everyone from *Fame Academy* and *Popstars: The Rivals* to record one happy Christmas charity singalong. His Bobness had the sense to turn the idea down flat.

'When the Going Gets Tough' by Boyzone
In which Ronan and the boys achieve the near-impossible feat of making Billy Ocean seem like some sort of soul legend. If only they'd covered 'Get Out of My Dreams, Get Into My Car'. *That* would have been comic relief.

'Just Say No' by The Grange Hill Cast
If only they had. We could have done without hearing this dreadful rally for anti-drug charity SKODA.

'Eine Kleine Lift Muzik' by Blur
The *Help!* album was a great idea. Bands record one song each in a day, stick them on a record in aid of War Child. Some ('Lucky' by Radiohead) were genius. Others, like this feeble instrumental effort, could've been given another twenty-four hours at least to sort out.

The Eleven Greatest Covers of All Time . . .

That's covers as in versions of other people's songs. Not that there's anything wrong with any of these record sleeves or anything . . .

'Nothing Compares 2 U' by Sinead O'Connor
A cover that was, simply, career-defining. With one fine Prince discard,

Sinead went from stroppy and scary to honest and heartfelt, helped by that video where the emotion of the moment made her cry. Great as Sinead's cover was, it made you think, what the hell was Prince doing, giving it away to *Paisley Park* nobodies The Family?

'Wonderwall' by Ryan Adams

At the other end of the spectrum to 'Nothing . . .' is Ryan Adams' cover of nineties ubiquity. Even Oasis are bored of the original version, playing it electrically instead; Noel has split up from its inspiration; Travis borrowed the chords for 'Driftwood'; and every busker knows the words. Full marks, then, to Ryan Adams for having the guts to tackle it on *Love is Hell* – and not only that, but also for having made it sound different and (dare one say it?) better.

'Smells Like Teen Spirit' by Tori Amos

If Ryan Adams made 'Wonderwall' gentler, but still kept its essence intact, Tori Amos took on 'Smells Like Teen Spirit' with nothing but a piano and stripped it down to its barest emotions. Again, as powerful as the original and then some, poignant rather than rocking, *and* you can hear the words.

'Nobody Does It Better' by Radiohead

We've never heard this version, which Radiohead covered for a TV special. But we think that's probably for the best, as it probably sounds so much better in your head. 'Creep' meets Carly Simon? Thanks very much. By not following it through, Radiohead avoided the pitfalls suffered by . . .

'Baby One More Time' by Travis

For this, the B-side to their 'Turn' single, Travis stripped Britney's anthem (not Britney – that would be rude) until it was acoustically strummed and switched from poppy to creepy. It highlighted how much 'Baby One More Time' is a great pop song, and at the same time gave Travis a party piece to perform as they did yet another radio interview in midwest America. They ended their set with it for a while, until the joke wore off.

'Whole Lotta Love' by Prince

'I'm not interested in what you know,' Prince told concerned-looking audiences during his 2002 tour. 'I'm interested in what you can learn.' But nestled in among the numerous funk workouts was this cover of the Led Zep classic. His band stripped down to drums and bass, Prince on storming guitar and singing the whole thing falsetto, it reduced grown men to gibbering wrecks. Seek it out.

'Mad World' by Michael Andrews featuring Gary Jules

Like Tori with 'Teen Spirit', Michael and Gary took an electro-pop hit and took it back to just piano and voice. It's like a different song. And, with its slightly spooky tone, perfect for the Christmas market. The UK number one Tears for Fears never had.

'All Along the Watchtower' by Jimi Hendrix
A slip of a song from Bob Dylan's *John Wesley Harding* that Hendrix put a stick of dynamite underneath and reinvented for *Electric Ladyland*. It wasn't the first time he'd covered Dylan – at Monterey, he'd had a stab at 'Like A Rolling Stone', only to forget the words halfway through – but this take was more successful, so much so that these days Dylan plays Hendrix's cover version, rather than his own original.

'Where the Streets Have No Name' by The Pet Shop Boys
This, remember, was before U2 discovered irony. Neil and Chris turned Adam's running bass and *The Joshua Tree*'s rock-out opening into a monotone, hi-energy, deadpan disco classic, seguing it into 'Can't Take My Eyes Off You'. U2 might have them on guitar, but this version, in our opinion, has the edge.

'Comfortably Numb' by The Scissor Sisters
Anything The Pet Shop Boys can do, The Scissor Sisters can do better. 'Where the Streets . . .' at least had something approaching a driving beat. Compare by contrast the original Pink Floyd version of 'Comfortably Numb'. What kind of musical genius listens to that stodge and thinks, 'Aha! There are the makings of a Hi-NRG classic here'? A greater mind by several divisions than our own. Genius.

'Hallelujah' by Jeff Buckley
Leonard Cohen did it originally. Jeff Buckley did it better. Leonard Cohen did it well. Jeff Buckley's version makes your jaw drop. Leonard Cohen's voice is low, contained, distinct. Jeff Buckley's voice is high and low, emotional, defining. Leonard Cohen is alive. Jeff Buckley, sadly, is dead.

And the Eleven Worst Covers of All Time

There's nothing wrong with these sleeves, either. At least, not compared to what is inside them.

'911 Is a Joke' by Duran Duran
In 1993 Duran Duran recorded *Thank You*, an album of eye-poppingly awful cover versions, each by a Duran inspiration. Some thanks. 'White

Lines' is still inexplicably hauled out on tour, but even more unbelievable is their cover of the Public Enemy song '911 Is a Joke', which really is not a joke. Except, of course, this cover is.

'How Soon Is Now?' by taTu
Confucius say, when teenage Russian lesbians tackle eighties miserable masterpiece, best to cover ears.

'Summer Holiday' by Kevin the Gerbil
Roland Rat's unfunny sidekick takes on Cliff classic. Anyone got the number for Rentokil?

'The Long and Winding Road' by Will and Gareth
Dear God, just *no*. The original version, mangled by Phil Spector at John Lennon's behest, is not a patch on how Paul McCartney wanted it (pared down as on *Let It Be, Naked*). But its OTT production seems the height of good taste compared to this *Pop Idol* double-header. One would hope that Will had enough sense to hate every minute of it, but was contractually obliged to go through with it. One would hope that Gareth was too bamboozled by Jordan's breasts to be thinking straight. Long. And Whiny.

'We Will Rock You' by 5ive
Not a great song in the first place, but 5ive (don't get us started on the name) managed to remove its last ounce of *joie de vivre* and turn its handclapping routine into half rock concert, half Nuremberg rally. Honest, watch the video. It's scary. The fact that they got Brian May to burst through a screen and squiggle at the end does not save their bacon.

'Knocking on Heaven's Door' by Guns N' Roses.
Pointless, painful and badly pronounced. The Roses just about got away with their cover of 'Live and Let Die', which at least contained some fireworks they could get hold of. But Axl's admittedly great rock voice just didn't suit the Bob classic. We say, knock it off.

'The Greatest Love of All' by Kevin Rowland
What the hell was Kevin Rowland doing covering Whitney Houston? And why, *why*, did he decide to talk the verses? It's every bit as bad as you can imagine.

'It's Raining Men' by Geri Halliwell
Firstly, it's a terrible song. Secondly, you can't substitute two big soul mamas for one tiny pop singer and expect to get away with it. But thirdly,

you can't have a crack at one bit of eighties pop culture and do a video that's based on another (*Flashdance*). That's just wrong.

'Born to Run' by Frankie Goes to Hollywood

For about twenty-five minutes, *Welcome to the Pleasuredome* sets its stall out as one of the great pop records of the eighties. But after the title track, 'Two Tribes' and 'Relax', Frankie and Trevor Horn run out of ideas. How else could the thought of covering Bruce Springsteen firstly arise, and then end up on the record? Bizarre.

'Baby One More Time' by Darius

As awful as Travis's version is brilliant. Darius did what can only be described as a free-form scat version of the Britney original in the first series of *Popstars*. Even despite this sterling effort, he wasn't considered bad enough to become a member of Hear'Say.

'Baby I Don't Care' by Jennifer Ellison

Who in their right mind could think that covering Transvision Vamp would be a good idea? Who could have thought that Wendy James could be made to sound half decent?

Eleven Songs that Classic Albums could Live Without

The joy of the iPod and the MP3 world is the ability to edit. And, even with 40GB of memory to fill, you're still going to want to save space by pruning the track that always makes you reach for the remote. In fact, why not burn the following eleven songs on to a CD and label it *The Songs I Never Want to Hear Again* . . .

'Yellow Submarine' by The Beatles

Revolver is, arguably, the greatest Beatles album, but let's be honest: how much better would it be if 'Yellow Submarine' was taken off and, say, 'Rain' was put on in its place? You'd be swapping Ringo for what he's crap at (singing) for what he's very good at (his finest drums performance). Save 'Yellow Submarine' for the *Yellow Submarine* soundtrack and leave the sound of sixties guitar perfection alone.

'Fitter, Happier' by Radiohead

Otherwise known as the bit where *OK Computer* becomes *Not OK*

Computer, as a sub-Hawking voice waffles its way through a load of mechanical *bons mots*. It's interesting once, and then it grates like buggery. And not only that, but it also breaks the album's sublime spell: before you know it, you're thinking, 'Actually, "Electioneering" is not so great either,' and you're skipping right through to 'Lucky'.

'Breaking into Heaven' by The Stone Roses

Or, more specifically, the first four minutes and thirty-six seconds of 'Breaking into Heaven', the opener of *The Second Coming*. It's just noise: birds, bongos, trains . . . You listen to it only once; on subsequent plays your finger hits 'skip' until the guitar kicks in. From that point on, the song's one of the best things the band ever did.

'Digsy's Diner' by Oasis

We could have said 'She's Electric' off *Morning Glory*, but, if truth be told, there are half a dozen tracks you can skip on the second greatest Oasis album. *Definitely Maybe*, however, contains just one clanger. Liam sings about lasagne. It's cheesy (particularly the way Digsy makes it) and quite rightly you want to head straight for 'Slide Away' instead.

'The Girl Is Mine' by Michael Jackson

For all his wacko behaviour, it should never be forgotten that with *Off the Wall* and *Thriller* Jacko is a ledge of the first order. However, even *Thriller* contains this clunker, with a little helping hand from Paul McCartney. Rather than arguing the toss over to whom the girl belonged, Jacko should have just said, 'Have her, Paul, I've got Billie Jean.'

'Come on Eileen' by Dexy's Midnight Runners

Each of the Dexy's albums – *Searching for the Young Soul Rebels, Too-Rye-Aye* and *Don't Stand Me Down* – are genius in their own right. But *Too-Rye-Aye* is ruined by the ubiquitous 'Eileen', which has simply been played to death and does not need to be heard by anyone, ever again. In a parallel universe it was never released as a single, and is a stand-out album track. In this universe, remove.

'Walk of Life' by Dire Straits

We won't ask why you've got *Brothers in Arms* in your collection. Don't worry, we know that in 1985 it was a compulsory purchase for the entire record-buying public. 'So Far Away' is bearable. 'Money for Nothing' is money for nothing. The title song even ended up on *The West Wing*. But 'Walk of Life'? Walk the plank, please.

'Ob-La-Di Ob-La-Da' by The Beatles

Even given that *The White Album* is a double album, there really isn't room for this song. The band played it once, and never wanted to hear it again. We say, to have got all the way to the end John must have been in a pretty good mood.

'New Orleans Instrumental No. 1' by REM

Automatic for the People is widely considered the band's masterpiece. The truth is that the opening run of songs is brilliant, the closing sequence bordering on genius, the middle section pants. And no more so than this dribbly instrumental that does nothing, says nothing and should have stayed on the studio floor.

'Rainy Day Women Nos 12 and 35' by Bob Dylan

Dylan makes a pun on the word 'stoned'. You have to be stoned to find this funny. Considering that his previous two albums started with 'Subterranean Homesick Blues' and 'Like a Rolling Stone' respectively, this is a weak successor. Once you're past it, *Blonde on Blonde* is a God-like creation.

Anything on *Wish You Were Here* that isn't 'Wish You Were Here' or 'Shine on You Crazy Diamond' by Pink Floyd

There are only five songs on *Wish You Were Here*, and two of those are 'Shine on' Parts One and Two. We say, erase the other two and treat the record for what it is: the greatest prog-rock double A-side of all time.

The Eleven Best 'Greatest Hits' Albums of All Time . . .

The 'greatest hits' album, or 'seeing out a contract', as it is sometimes known, is a staple of the music industry, particularly around Christmas. But for all their cash-in qualities, some become defining records in their own right.

Carry On Up the Charts: The Best of The Beautiful South

The Beautiful South had always done OK, ticked over nicely, thank you very much, but when a 'greatest hits' album was released, the nation couldn't help but splash out. There is some scary statistic about how one in five British households own this record. The really scary thing is, it might be even more.

Recurring Dream: The Very Best of Crowded House
'You know more Crowded House songs than you think you do', ran the strap-line on the adverts. Clearly the nation didn't know them well enough. A band of not many hits but numerous great songs, the nation once again couldn't resist.

Abba: Gold
You need only one Abba record, don't you? One with all the hits on. Simply and elegantly packaged, the band's defining record rocked up more than a decade after the band split up. Thank you for the music, said a grateful nation.

Ladies and Gentlemen: The Best of George Michael
Similarly, this is the only George Michael record you really need. Firstly, it's the one where he's got a sense of humour. And secondly, he's helpfully themed the two discs, one for the 'heart' and one for the 'feet'. We say, bin the first and turn up the second.

1962–1966 (*The Red Album*) by The Beatles
In the sixties, singles had a habit of not appearing on albums. Which makes this compilation of early Beatles' songs up there with their best records.

1967–1970 (*The Blue Album*) by The Beatles
Same photo as the red cover but with longer hair. Fewer songs about holding hands, but more about walruses.

Hot Rocks 1964–71 by The Rolling Stones
Forget the material, corking that it is. That weird hairy silhouette thing with everyone's head inside each other's is worth the money alone.

12 Gold Bars by Status Quo
One of these writers is intimately acquainted with this record, having heard it every day on the school bus for the best part of two years. Be honest, it rocks.

Greatest Hits by Queen
Like *12 Gold Bars*, this collection stops before the eighties starts and is all the better for it. All the Queen you'll ever need to own.

The Immaculate Collection by Madonna
This collection, meanwhile, does the decent thing by stopping at the end of the eighties. 'American Pie' need not apply.

Remasters by Led Zeppelin
How many other 'greatest hits' can you think of that are triple albums?

And the Eleven Most Pointless 'Greatest Hits' Albums of All Time

Some artists, however, have no need for the summing-up CD . . .

Super Hits by Blue Öyster Cult
Can songs that didn't chart be called a hit, let alone a super hit? It's not the Reaper you need to fear, it's the rest of this album.

The Best of It Bites
One bona fide Top Forty hit. *Calling all the Zeroes* might have been a better title?

Feels Like I'm in Love: The Best of Kelly Marie
Anagrammatically correct. *The Best of Kelly Marie* is *Feels Like I'm in Love.* The rest, frankly, isn't.

The Best of Fairground Attraction
Fairground Attraction had one best-selling album, *The First of a Million Kisses.* It's pretty good. So good, in fact, that their 'best of' plunders nine songs from it.

The Very Best of The Stone Roses
The very best of The Stone Roses is, of course, *The Stone Roses.* Buy that. If you're feeling optimistic, buy *The Second Coming.* Don't bother with this.

The Best of Vanilla Ice
A slightly meagre ten songs here, but even on this limited volume the hit-to-track ratio is still only 2:8.

Hammer: The Hits
You can, if you so wish, buy a double pack of Vanilla Ice and MC Hammer. The hit-to-track ratio is now up to a mega-value 3:7.

Greatest Hits III by Queen
Queen's *Greatest Hits* is great. Queen's *Greatest Hits II* is passable. Queen's

Greatest Hits III includes the solo work of Brian May. Neither great nor, technically, Queen.

Greatest Hits by Tiffany
The phrase 'greatest hits' implies an artist struggling to decide which of many smashes should make the final cut. For Tiffany, the question was how to spread the four of them out.

The Best of The Primitives
There are sixteen songs here. They had three Top Thirty hits.

The Best of The Cutting Crew
Which is two more than this lot managed.

Eleven Albums Everyone Owns

Forget So Solid, *this* is the real garage music: CDs bought on impulse in motorway service stations up and down the country. You may not even remember exactly when or why you bought them, but they are the seeds of dirt around which all record collections, like pearls, accrue. A skilled archaeologist, or Tony Robinson, can skim through a record rack and use these markers to date – sometimes to within a month – the moment when the subject was introduced to the record-shop habit.

Fear those whose record collection consists entirely of Default Albums, for they will undoubtedly consider the rugby shirt to be acceptable casual-wear and will inevitably recommend a lovely little pub by the river in Richmond. Indeed, he or she will almost certainly be Jeremy Clarkson. Here then are the eleven middle-of-the-road classics that everyone owns. Even you.

Dark Side of the Moon by Pink Floyd
Almost synonymous with the term 'hi-fi demo disc'.

Led Zeppelin IV
It's got 'Stairway' on it.

No Jacket Required by Phil Collins
When demented maverick Peter Gabriel left Genesis, no one expected the remaining muso geeks to make a go of it. The idea that *two* of them (Collins and Mike Rutherford) would then go on to achieve massive success was, frankly, unthinkable.

Rumours by Fleetwood Mac
Like settling into a bath of warm Bailey's, this was the true sound of 1977.

Bat Out of Hell by Meat Loaf
For many, the sole sanctuary from the rigours of punk rock. For many others, the definition of overblown pomp.

Blue Lines by Massive Attack
By the end of the eighties, everyone in England – except the Queen Mum and the authors of this volume – had smoked at least one joint. This is the result.

Brothers in Arms by Dire Straits
An album that, while still accepted as 'new wave' by contemporary listeners, was the yuppie choice of the midi hi-fi age.

The War of the Worlds by Jeff Wayne
In the last years of the 1970s, little did we know that music was being made on a mixing desk far more powerful than our own.

No Angel by Dido
This is a Faithless album with the funk removed for your safety.

Moon Safari by Air
The sound made by a River Café cookbook being opened.

The Blue Album/The Red Album by The Beatles
EMI thoughtfully distill all the clever bits of the Scouse legends' career, all the better to fit them into the nation's glove compartment.

Eleven Great Eleventh Tracks on Albums

Suede's Brett Anderson has a theory that every great album has a great seventh song. We say, seven, schmeven. The only track that matters is the one after number ten . . .

'I am the Resurrection' by The Stone Roses
Classic debut album saves the best until eleventh.

'Under the Bridge' by The Red Hot Chili Peppers
Blood, sugar, sex and magic, all in one eleventh song.

'I Just Wasn't Made for these Times' by The Beach Boys
The *Pet Sounds'* pet sound.

'In My Life' by The Beatles
You have to have a rubber soul to not be affected by this.

'It's All Over Now, Baby Blue' by Bob Dylan
The Bobster brings *Bringing it All Back Home* back home.

'Amsterdam' by Coldplay
The song that gives us a rush of blood to the head.

'From the Morning' by Nick Drake
Troubled singer's final album ends on an up note.

'Night Swimming' by REM
An automatic for the people choice.

'There, There, My Dear' by Dexy's Midnight Runners
Kevin stole our laptop until we agreed to put this song on the list.

'The Asphalt World' by Suede
Brit-prog wig-out on the stand-out track from *Dog Man Star*.

'Are You Experienced?' by The Jimi Hendrix Experience
Well, are you?

Eleven Beatles Tribute Albums

Some fab and some not.

All This and World War Two
At the height of punk, not everyone was listening to The Sex Pistols. Who needed 'Pretty Vacant' when you could have Leo Sayer singing 'I am the Walrus', or Status Quo rocking through 'Getting Better'?

The Lennon and McCartney Songbook – Volume 2
'Help!' by Deep Purple. Help indeed.

Al Koso Wa Subete
The Beatles in Japanese. There's even a karaoke version of 'All You Need is Love'.

The Best of The Beatles' Songs Sung by Motown's Greatest Stars
Does exactly what it says on the tin. Diana Ross has a wander down 'The Long and Winding Road'. Martha Reeves adds her own little 'Something'.

Blue Beat: Blue Note Plays the Best of Lennon and McCartney
Anything Motown can do, Blue Note can do better. There's some decent stuff here, and there's Bobby McFerrin on 'From Me to You'.

The Exotic Beatles – Volume 1
Oh, dear God: Brian Sewell does a spoken-word version of 'I Wanna Be Your Man' and Derek Enright MP has a stab at 'Yellow Submarine'. In Latin.

Cello Submarine – Beatles' Classics by the Cellists of the Berlin Philharmonic
We're not making this up.

Bugs Bunny and Friends Sing The Beatles
If only that *was* all, folks. Elmer Fudd sings 'The Fool on the Hill'. Road Runner beep-beeps his way along 'The Long and Winding Road'.

François Glorieux Plays The Beatles
. . . in the style of classical composers. Here's 'Yesterday' in the style of Chopin. 'Ob-La-Di Ob-La-Da' rewritten to suit Mozart. Roll over, Beethoven.

The Beatle Barkers
You guessed it. Doggies sing all of your Beatle favourites. Hey, bulldog!

The Exotic Beatles – Volume 2
There's more. A hillbilly version of 'Let it Be' by The Squirrels. And Brian Sewell again, this time talking his way through 'Sgt. Pepper'.

Eleven Great Official Live Albums

There's the confines of the studio. And there's the slightly out-of-sync roar of the crowd . . .

No Sleep 'Til Hammersmith by Motörhead
In a word, loud.

Jimi Plays Monterey by Jimi Hendrix
'Killing Floor' is, in the authors' opinion, the best start to a record *ever*.
And then he set fire to his guitar.

Live 1966: The Royal Albert Hall Concert by Bob Dylan
It's not just Bob who's electric – the audience are, too.

Live at the Apollo, Volume One by James Brown
The record-company boss didn't want to release it. The record-company
boss was, frankly, mad.

Songs of Faith and Devotion Live by Depeche Mode
It's the same songs as *Songs of Faith and Devotion*, in the same order,
played the same way. For such sheer chutzpah, we salute.

Pulse by Pink Floyd
This one, meanwhile, contains the whole of *Dark Side of the Moon*. Plus
a box with a little beepy light on it.

Texas Campfire Tapes by Michelle Shocked
Michelle Shocked, at a campfire, recorded on a cassette player. If only life
was always this simple.

Under a Blood Red Sky by U2
Red-meat rock at Red Rocks, Arizona. No rebel songs.

Weld by Neil Young
Forget the actual album, great that it is. Listen to the accompanying CD,
Arc: nothing more and nothing less than a load of feedback.

Rank by The Smiths
Marr persuaded Morrissey to let him have a second guitarist for this tour.
The result was 'How Soon is Rock'.

Live at Leeds by The Who
Five tracks. Windmills aplenty.

SPLIFFS AND STIFFS

Eleven Rock-Star Druggies

Remember, kids: hugs, not drugs.

Paul McCartney
Macca was arrested at Tokyo International airport by customs officials who found 219 grams of marijuana in his suitcases. He was taken to the Tokyo narcotics headquarters, handcuffed and had a rope tied around him. At first Macca thought the jail was barbaric but 'underneath the guards were quite warm . . . I got a few requests for "Yesterday" – it was a bit of a laugh.' One suspects that had he sung 'Mull of Kintyre' he would have been released sooner.

Bobby Brown
In addition to drug arrests, Whitney Houston's husband has been arrested variously for sexual battery, drunken driving, violation of parole, not paying fees on time, not submitting to a drug test, and generally being a naughty boy. He said recently, 'I have a disease. I am an addict. I am an alcoholic. Hopefully I can get back to what I do best – dancing and singing.' Oh dear.

Steve Kilbey
The lead singer of veteran Australian rock band The Church was arrested in New York for allegedly attempting to buy heroin. He managed to joke that 'a drug bust is something every ageing rock star should have under his belt'. His band, feeling rather peeved at being without a singer the night before, didn't bail him out.

Joe Cocker
After a concert in Adelaide in 1972, Cocker got high with a little help from booze and marijuana. He was arrested, pleaded guilty and was bailed for A$1,000. In Melbourne five days later, he unwisely yelled out, 'In five years marijuana will be legalized and the same cat who is trying to throw us out now will be smoking it himself.' Unimpressed immigration minister Jim Forbes gave Cocker four hours to leave the country.

Courtney Love
She pleaded guilty to twelve drug-possession charges after breaking windows outside her boyfriend's house and then overdosed on Oxycontin in front of her daughter, Frances Bean. In March 2004, she faced two felony charges for possession of a controlled substance and lost $55,000 in bail for not turning up to court on an unrelated assault charge. She was recently admitted to a medical facility in California for an 'emergency gynaecological condition'. This is the same woman who once said, 'If there's any time you should be on drugs it's when you're pregnant 'cause it sucks.'

Elvis Presley
The King played an important role in trying to curb the drug excesses of the US public in general and, by example, the rock community specifically. In 1970 in full-on Elvis garb, he turned up at the White House and requested an audience with President Nixon. By lunchtime he had been made an honorary agent in the Drug Enforcement Agency. One suspects Elvis thought that once he was part of the Establishment he'd be above the law – useful, given his addiction to prescription drugs. Only in America.

James Brown
In 1988, the Godfather of Soul was convicted of threatening behaviour after a cross-state chase. After serving fifteen months in jail, his good conduct got him moved to a reintegration centre. He made public-service announcements warning against alcohol and drug abuse before being finally released in February 1991 on the condition that he neither drove nor possessed firearms. So far so good, so good, so good.

Boy George
He famously declared that 'I'm a drag addict, not a drug addict' and teased the press by calling himself 'your favourite junkie'. Following successful treatment for his dependence on drugs – primarily heroin – he publicly denounced them and embarked on a solo career. As he once said, 'I've only got one criminal record: "Karma Chameleon".'

David Crosby
In 2004, Crosby was arrested on marijuana- and gun-possession charges in a Times Square hotel in New York and was eventually charged with criminal possession of a weapon in the third degree, a felony, and illegal possession of a hunting knife, ammunition and marijuana. He pleaded guilty and was fined $5,000. Why take one charge into court when you

can take a whole bunch? The man should be rewarded for his saving of police time.

Keith Richards
Richards has kept dealers, doctors and policemen pretty busy over the years. In 1977, Canadian Mounties got in on the act when they arrested him in a Montreal hotel for possession of heroin – once they had managed to wake him up. As Keef once said, 'I took drugs because I wanted to hide . . . Life was just too bloody public, and that was the only place where I could handle it . . . Eventually you realize it's self-defeating – especially heroin.'

Shane MacGowan
In November 1999 ex-Pogues singer MacGowan, the musician least likely to front a toothpaste commercial, was arrested on suspicion of possession of a class-A drug after the police found him unconscious in his flat. Only someone as totally wasted as Shane could convince himself (and everybody who helped it reach number two) that a song aimed at the Christmas market should contain lines such as 'Happy Christmas your arse I pray to God it's our last'. Huge hit though.

Eleven 'Legal' Highs*

Alcohol
The main psychoactive ingredient in alcoholic beverages is ethanol, which results from the fermentation of sugar by yeast. Ups: The whole world is your best mate. Downs: Quietly, please.

Ayahuasca
A vine native to the Amazon basin and containing alkaloids. Ups: Mental clouding, hallucinations with colourful visions. Downs: Trembling and sweating; large doses may depress the central nervous system.

Coffee
An addictive, overpriced dark liquid. Ups: Zing-zing-zing! Downs: Headaches, fatigue or drowsiness. Limit your intake to 200–300 mg of caffeine per day.

* Local restrictions may apply. If in doubt, check with a friendly policeman and/or a good lawyer.

Datura
A plant that grows wild in India, Mexico and the US and contains hyoscine and atropine. Ups: Euphoria, visual distortion, hallucinations and sleep. Intoxication can last from a few hours to many days. Downs: Your heart is at risk if you use it for too long and you could suffer from sluggishness.

Damiana
A shrub found in Mexico and Central/Southern America. Ups: A mild sixty-minute euphoria – it may even make you feel a bit sexy. Downs: Not good for your lungs – don't smoke it. May give you the runs.

Guarana
A Brazilian berry containing Guarine. Ups: It's a mild stimulant, which will keep you awake. Downs: Stay away if you have heart problems or high blood pressure.

Ephedrine
An extract of the Chinese herb Ma Huang. Ups: Stimulant effects, such as shivers up and down the spine, sensitive skin and muscles, and feelings of exhilaration. Downs: Muscle spasms and, er, heart attacks.

Wormwood
Like absinthe. Ups: Narcotic-like effects, vivid dreams. Downs: When taken in excess, it can cause tremors, convulsions, miscarriage, paralysis, stomach problems, and brain damage.

Yohimbe
Found in the bark and roots of a tree which grows in the Cameroon and Zaire. Ups: It's mildly hallucinogenic and it may make you feel 'up for it'. Downs: Everything going, from nausea and irritability through to racing heartbeat and depression.

Holy Sage
A soft-leaved Mexican plant. Ups: Colourful hallucinations. Downs: Headaches, irritability and the triggering of latent psychological problems. Doh!

Sex
What is it? No idea – we're all married. *Active ingredient?* Usually the male. Ups: Hopefully. Downs: Possibly, but never with the lights on and not on a Sunday.

Eleven Songs that are Definitely Maybe Not about Drugs, Actually

'Golden Brown' by The Stranglers
It had a texture like sun, gorgeous string arrangements and a soaring melody but was probably about heroin. Well, the *Daily Mail* tried to get it banned, but succeeded only in making it a massive hit. If you read the lyrics very carefully you'll see that it's a bit vague, but you never know.

'Lucy in the Sky with Diamonds' by The Beatles
Lucy + Sky + Diamonds just has to mean LSD, doesn't it? Not according to John Lennon, who insisted that the initials in the title were a coincidence – it actually came from a picture his son Julian had painted about his school friend, which Julian had named 'Lucy in the sky with diamonds'. John said: 'I swear to God, or swear to Mao, or to anybody you like, I had no idea it spelt LSD.' Oh right – sorry to have bothered you, then. And could we just ask you about your song 'Cold Turkey'? Oh, deep-frozen poultry, you say? Really?

'Ebeneezer Goode' by The Shamen
Not based on the little-known Dickens novel *The Tale Of Ebeneezer Goode*, we think.

'Pass the Dutchie' by Musical Youth
Any resemblance to The Mighty Diamonds' song 'Pass the Kouchie' ('kouchie' being Jamaican patois for pipe of marijuana) is obviously an extraordinary coincidence. They said on TV that it was about a saucepan which needed to be passed around on the left-hand side. More rice, anyone?

'Puff the Magic Dragon' by Peter, Paul and Mary
He lived by the sea and there was a connection with a land called Hona Lee, we seem to remember. There may even have been some frolicking at some point. Lots of people think it is about puff but Peter Yarrow gets cross when that's suggested.

'Purple Haze' by Jimi Hendrix
It may be about LSD, or it may be about marijuana. It's certainly not about air-freshener.

'Stairway to Heaven' by Led Zeppelin
Mr Plant says that it was inspired by *The Hobbit*, but we say it describes the downward spiral of a heroin addict's life. Or it's a Thora Hird-inspired remix of the Stannah Stair Lift theme tune.

'Marrakesh Express' by Crosby, Stills and Nash
Is this the same Mr Crosby who a few pages ago was arrested for possession of cannabis, a knife and a gun? Thought so.

'Eight Miles High' by The Byrds
Not about easyJet.

'Snowblind' by Black Sabbath
Not about Captain Scott's finest hour.

'Teletubbies Say "Eh-Oh!"' by The Teletubbies
A searing indictment of the effects that hallucinogenic drugs can have on a fragmented society. No question about it.

Eleven Rock 'n' Roll Deaths

As every rock star knows, the more rock 'n' roll your exit from Planet Rock, the better. Some stars got it right and some stars just . . . well . . . didn't.

Elvis Presley
By the time Elvis died he was the biggest star in the world in terms of weight alone. Looking like an avocado in Lycra, he was found dead with traces of fourteen different drugs in his body, with his trousers round his ankles, facing forward, *not* actually on the loo but certainly having fallen forward *off* it. Verdict: Blushworthy.

Dennis Wilson
This would be funny were it not true. Actually, on reflection, it is still pretty funny. The only Beach Boy who actually surfed, Dennis drowned after diving from his yacht in California. Can you guess where his family chose to bury him? Yup – at sea. Verdict: Hilarious vibrations.

Buddy Holly
On 3 February 1959, Holly's chartered plane – the *American Pie* – crashed, killing him, the Big Bopper and Ritchie Valens. The following items were recovered from the wreckage: Holly's glasses, Valens' crucifix and the Bopper's dice. Poignant, or what? Verdict: The day the music died. Sad – if only Madonna hadn't spoilt the memory.

John Lennon
Lennon was gunned down by Mark Chapman outside the Dakota Building

in New York on 8 December 1980. Chapman said he did it because 'I took it upon myself to judge him falsely for being in a lotus position with a flower, and I got angry in my stupidity.' Parole was denied, amazingly. Verdict: Tragic.

Mama Cass

Ms 'California Dreamin'' is commonly believed to have choked to death on a ham sandwich but in fact boringly died from a massive heart attack caused by her obesity. That hasn't stopped the Psych-a-deli in Marietta, USA, creating a tasteful tribute – the 'Mama Cass sandwich' ($7), which comprises a thick slice of homemade meatloaf between sourdough bread, served with a deli pickle and your choice of chips. Verdict: Can I supersize that?

Jimi Hendrix

On the morning of 18 September 1970, apparently after nothing more than a late-night tuna sandwich, Jimi's girlfriend found him dead in bed. Cause of death was later recorded as 'inhalation of vomit after barbiturate intoxication'. There is no report of the Psych-a-deli adding a Jimi Hendrix to their menu at this time. Verdict: At least it was his own vomit.

Marc Bolan

What lesson can we learn from the career of Marc Bolan, the architect of glam rock, the grandfather of punk rock? Simply that, if it is four a.m. and you are knackered and scared of cars, you should probably wait for a night bus. On 16 September 1977, he was killed when his girlfriend's car hit a tree at a notorious accident blackspot on Barnes Common while travelling at a rocktastic 30mph. Verdict: Embarrassing.

Jim Morrison

Morrison took loads of drugs, caused audience hysteria wherever he played and even drank his partner's blood at a pagan wedding. On the morning of 3 July 1971, in Paris, his girlfriend found him dead in the bath. Although the cause of death was reportedly 'heart failure', some rumours persist that he masturbated himself to death – though it's also said that he isn't dead at all and is now living in Mexico. (Why is it always Mexico?) Verdict: A clean jerk.

Brian Jones

Jones was sacked by The Stones in 1969 for being a 'total liability'. He cut down on the drugs and started to restore his country estate – once the home of A. A. Milne – but became involved in a wrangle with his builders over bills and eventually, after a scuffle, ended up dead at the bottom of his pool. Theories abound but we can exclusively reveal that reports of a game of Pooh sticks going badly wrong are lies. Verdict: He should have got more than one estimate.

Michael Hutchence

The INXS front-man had it all – including Kylie – before settling down with Paula Yates, with whom he had a daughter. But her other children became the subjects of endless custody battles which rapidly became a public nightmare as Yates and Hutchence fought the children's father, the unassailable 'Saint' Bob Geldof. What happened at the end is inconclusive – Hutchence was found hanging in his hotel room in what many thought was an autoerotic act, but the coroner favoured the verdict of suicide. Paula was to follow. Verdict: Elegantly wasted indeed.

Janis Joplin

Joplin enjoyed fist-fights with Hell's Angels, drunken appearances on television and general out-of-control behaviour. It would never happen today, would it, Courtney? Janis was careful about her drugs, though, and always bought from a dealer who had his stuff checked by a chemist. Presumably said chemist's was closed on the day she took her fatal dose of heroin. Verdict: Rock 'n' roll.

Eleven Feel-Good Death-Metal Albums

Death metal was born in the USA during the 1980s with the emergence of subtly named bands such as The Chasm, Cannibal Corpse, Morbid Angel, the checky popular beat combo Suffocation and the delightful Entombed. The tempo is turbo-charged anarchy, with screaming guitars, thrashing drums, growling vocals and songs that aren't ever going to feature on *Pop Idol* or be given away as a *Cosmo* cover-mount. If you could invent a death-metal metronome it wouldn't be visible to the human eye and it would come in only one colour – black. And the lyrical content? When veterans Malevolent Creation released their album *The Fine Art of Murder* (the follow-up to their classic *Stillborn*), lead guitarist Phil Fasciana said, 'The first three albums were dedicated to death, or stories about death and ways of death.'

Nice one. No chance of a collaboration with S Club, then?

So next time a 'supper party' you're hosting goes on too long, chuck out the Dido, the Enya and the Norah J and put a selection of the following on your autochanger. They definitely won't stay for coffee . . .

Reign in Blood by Slayer

Master of Puppets by Metallica

Among the Living by Anthrax

Game Over by Nuclear Assault

Controlled by Hatred by Suicidal Tendencies

Soul of a New Machine by Fear Factory

Necroticism – Descanting the Insalubrious by Carcass

Clandestine by Entombed

Kill 'Em All by Metallica

Need to Control by Brutal Truth

Rape of the Bastard Nazarene by Akercocke
(It was a toss-up between this album and their new disc, *Choronzon*, which has been described as 'faster, heavier, more disturbing and much fucking nastier'.)

You've got to admire the coherency of the message. Black, none more black.

Suicide isn't Painless: Eleven Songs to Slit Your Throat To (Parts One and Two)

(PART ONE) ELEVEN SONGS TO GET YOU IN THE MOOD

Obviously, kids, our recommendation is that you call The Samaritans or your mum. But if you *are* set on suicide, here's our suggested soundtrack.

'Heaven Knows I'm Miserable Now' by The Smiths

'Suicide is Painless', the theme from *M*A*S*H*

'Stan' by Eminem

'Mad World' by Tears for Fears (the Michael Andrews featuring Gary Jules version)

'Dead Souls' by Joy Division (RIP Ian Curtis)

'Song Sung Blue' by Altered Images

'Polly' by Nirvana

'Everybody Hurts' by REM

'Sad Songs (They Say So Much)' by Elton John

'With or Without You' by U2

'Bridge Over Troubled Water' by Simon and Garfunkel

If you would rather hang on in there for a while but fancy doing some research, check out the following.

(PART TWO) ELEVEN SONGS ABOUT SUICIDE

'Steelbath Suicide' by Soilwork

'Sk8er Boi' by Avril Lavigne

'Suicide Machine' by No Fun At All

'Richard Hung Himself' by Slayer

'Adam's Song' by Blink-182

'Suicide' by R Kelly

'Teenage Suicide' by Unwritten Law

'Hold On' by Good Charlotte

'Suicide' by Day Glo Abortions

Anything from John Vanderslice's 1999 album *Mass Suicide Occult Figurines*

'Don't Try Suicide' by Queen

Eleven Kurt Cobain Murder Clues

In April 1994, Seattle police arrived at the grunge icon and Nirvana front-man Kurt Cobain's house after a gardener found the greenhouse locked and saw a dead body inside.

Cobain's death triggered more than 100 copycat suicides from teen fans – yet while suicide was accepted as the official verdict, conspiracy theorists went mad. Here are eleven reasons why they think it was murder.

The suicide note
Experts say that there are two people's handwriting on the note. It has been said that the words 'Dear Boddah' at the start of the letter (Boddah was Kurt's childhood imaginary friend) and four lines at the end of the letter do not appear to be in Kurt's handwriting. Only the last four lines of the letter mention suicide.

The other note
Police reported that a second suicide note, signed 'Kurt Colbain' (sic) and addressed to Courtney, was found in a flowerpot by the door of the greenhouse. They said that both the misspelling of his own name and the oddity of two suicide notes were of 'no significance'.

His family
None of his blood relatives nor his lawyer thought he harboured suicidal tendencies.

The drugs
Kurt's blood contained three times the lethal dosage of heroin for an addict and seventy-five times the lethal dosage for someone who was 'clean'. With so much heroin inside him he wouldn't have been able to put all his drug paraphernalia away and then pull the trigger – he would have been almost instantly unconscious.

The scene
The policeman who discovered the body initially said that a stool had been wedged up against the door. However, it was later discovered that the greenhouse door had been unlocked.

The lack of gore
Little damage was done to Kurt's face. There was certainly none of the carnage you would expect from a point-blank shotgun blast.

The gun
According to friends, Kurt bought the gun before checking into rehab because he 'feared for his life'. No legible fingerprints were found on the gun.

The ammo
The ejected shotgun shell was found to the left of the body – not on the right, where it should have been, given the position Kurt was lying in. Also, three shots were loaded from a box of twenty-five. Who loads three shells if they're planning to kill themselves? Wouldn't one shell do it?

The credit card
Someone else was using Kurt's credit card after his death. A number of charges were made to the card in the days following his death but ceased once his body was discovered.

The pen
The pen used to write the suicide note had no fingerprints on it.

The hit-man
When interviewed by Nick Broomfield for his movie *Kurt and Courtney*, rock singer Eldon Hoke revealed that he had been offered $50,000 to kill Kurt. On 19 April 1997, eight days after he spoke to Broomfield, Hoke was found dead in Riverside, California.

Smells like this one will run and run.

Eleven Songs and a Funeral (Parts One and Two)

(PART ONE) TEN SONGS TO MAKE THE TEARS FLOW

What music should be playing when your loved ones pay their last respects, before they go off to get pissed and fight? Our friends at the Co-Operative Group's Funeral Services said that in 2002 sixty-eight per cent of their branches had reported an increase in the number of requests for pop music. Their Top Ten (luddites!) was as follows:

'Wind Beneath My Wings' by Bette Midler

'My Heart Will Go On' by Celine Dion

'I Will Always Love You' by Whitney Houston

'The Best' by Tina Turner

'Angels' by Robbie Williams
(As chosen for the funeral of the late great charity worker Mr Ronald Kray, apparently.)

'You'll Never Walk Alone' by Gerry and the Pacemakers

'Candle in the Wind' by Elton John

'Unchained Melody' by The Righteous Brothers

'Bridge Over Troubled Water' by Simon and Garfunkel

'Time to Say Goodbye' by Sarah Brightman

(PART TWO) ELEVEN LAUGH-OUT-LOUD FUNERAL SONGS

We thought their ideas rather boring. Here are our suggestions instead . . .

'Fire' by The Crazy World of Arthur Brown

'Ashes to Ashes' by David Bowie

'Bat Out of Hell' by Meat Loaf

'It's Oh So Quiet' by Björk

'Another One Bites the Dust' by Queen

'Living in a Box' by Black Box

'Going Underground' by The Jam

'I Will Survive' by Gloria Gaynor

'Wake Me Up Before You Go-Go' by Wham!

'I'm Outlived by *That* Thing?' by The Crash Test Dummies

'If You're Happy and You Know It Clap Your Hands', traditional song

Amen.

Eleven Things that Suggest that Elvis Lives

A recent sighting of Elvis made us worry, so we have mounted a full investigation on your behalf:

The headstone
Elvis's middle name (Aaron) is wrongly spelt (Aron) on his headstone.

The resting place
Elvis's resting place is not next to his mother's, where he had requested it to be.

The death certificate
Though he weighed about 250 lbs at the time of his death, his death certificate lists him at a spry 170 lbs. The original death certificate disappeared, and the current death certificate is dated two months after his alleged death.

The coffin
The coffin was suspiciously heavy, leading some to believe that it contained an air-conditioning unit to keep a wax body cool.

The funeral
This was held quickly to make it difficult for fans to attend, prompting conspiracy theorists to ask; could there have been concerns about fans recognizing flaws in a replica body?

The face
The body in the coffin had a pug nose and arched eyebrows (unlike Elvis) and most importantly, one of the sideburns on the 'corpse' was loose and falling off.

The hands
Elvis was an eighth-degree karate black belt whose hands were rough and callused; the hands of the body in the coffin were soft and pudgy.

The sighting
Two hours after Elvis's body was discovered, a man who looked remarkably like him purchased a plane ticket for Buenos Aires; he paid in cash and booked under the name John Burrows – the alias Elvis had used several times before.

The missing treasures
Elvis's prized possessions, most importantly Chiro's *Book of Numbers* and *The Autobiography of Yogi*, disappeared and were never recovered after his death.

The gift
The day after Elvis's death, Lucy De Barbon, his ex-lover, received in the mail a single rose from 'El Lancelot'. This had been her pet name for Elvis, and it was a name that no one else knew.

The numbers
He died on 16 August 1977. By adding together the numbers in that date, 8, 16 and 1,977, you get 2,001. *2001* is the title of Elvis's favourite movie, and its hero plans his immortality in the bathroom.

No doubt by the time this book comes out Elvis will be back and headlining the next Here and Now tour with Buddy Holly (who is planning his comeback from Mexico), Kurt Cobain (who is apparently living in Puerto Rico) and John Lennon (who is alive and well and living on the Internet at www.triumphpc.com/john-lennon-project).

Anyone who can prove that Elvis is alive should email juanlauda@rockandpopelevens.com and they will receive an all-expenses paid trip to Bill Beeny's Elvis Is Alive Museum and 50's Cafe, Interstate 70 in Wright City (not open Tuesdays). Conditions apply.

Cash After Death: Eleven Stars who Couldn't Take It with Them

Dying is often a brilliant career move and can really enhance your worth. Here are our eleven dead-rich stars who keep counting the cash from beyond the grave . . .

Eva Cassidy
American songbird Cassidy released only two albums during her short life. A year after her death from cancer her posthumously released third album, *Eva by Heart*, began to capture the public imagination as a result of passionate championing by BBC Radio Two's Terry Wogan, and eventually reached number one in the UK and Ireland. Her popularity crossed back

over the Atlantic to get her to the top of the Billboard chart. She has now sold more than 4 million records and has reached triple-platinum status.

Jerry Garcia
Long after Garcia's death, The Grateful Dead continue to release album after album, all of which get snapped up in their millions. The Grateful Dead merchandise – everything from T-shirts and dog bowls to sports bras – brings in some $30 million a year, which Jerry Garcia's estate shares with his former bandmates. Whether or not his estate gets a royalty from sales of Cherry Garcia ice-cream isn't clear.

Buddy Holly
His roster of hits has helped to generate huge sums in recent years. Sales have topped 40 million and spawned a massive hit film, an annual festival and museum at his birthplace of Lubbock, Texas, and a long-running West End stage musical. Our favourite merchandise choices include the Buddy Holly kazoo and the Buddy Holly torch (a very reasonable $6.00). No model Cessna planes, strangely.

Jimi Hendrix
A nasty legal case between the Hendrix family's lawyer, Leo Branton, and Hendrix's stepsister and father was settled in 1995. Since then things have blossomed and more than a dozen official Hendrix albums are now available. There is loads of merchandise adding to the coffers, including Purple Haze incense. There is even talk of a Hendrix action figure! With flame effect?

Janis Joplin
Her most famous album, the poignant and honest *Pearl*, wasn't released until after her death. The single 'Me and Bobby McGee' subsequently reached the top of the charts and there is till-clanking merchandise-a-plenty to choose from – from the Kosmic T-shirt to a ceramic music box based on the 1965 Porsche 356cc Cabriolet that was custom painted for Janis. Sadly no Mercedes Benz, though.

John Lennon and George Harrison
Beatles records regularly sell 2 million plus per year. There are enough cover versions around to fill a book of their own, John's solo albums have all sold consistently well and there has also been renewed interest in George's solo work since his death. When Liverpool becomes European City of Culture in 2008, the tills are bound to ring even louder.

Bob Marley
Legend is the best-selling reggae album of all time and the cheeky rasta is a global icon. There have been a crop of remixes and cover versions

since his death, and the line of available merchandise ranges from soccer shoes to rucksacks made of something called 'hemp'. Marley's influence has even reached the *Rock and Pop Elevens* postroom, where Gloria Dawson named our photocopier 'Bob' after him – 'It's always jammin'.'

Elvis Presley

Seventeen million Americans have at some point impersonated the King and Elvis has also cleverly been able to endorse a large number of products from beyond the grave – among them Lipton Brisk Iced Tea, Energizer batteries, Toyota cars and Apple computers. *Forbes* magazine's annual Dead Rich Celebrities list estimates that Elvis earns a stunning $40 million a year.

Tupac Shakur

Shakur, who died aged twenty-five in a still-unsolved drive-by shooting, was controversial, rich and influential. Many of the hundreds of his recordings that were never released during his life have appeared on eight posthumous albums which have generated more than $6 million for his estate – the net worth of which has increased to an estimated $60 million since his death, according to *Black Wealth and Fortunes* magazine.

Frank Sinatra

The original stadium rocker Ol' Blue Eyes was nominated for a posthumous Grammy in 2001 for his 'duet' with Celine Dion. Last year he sold almost 3 million albums and there is no doubt that the jazz/big band revival has sent people scurrying back to the recordings of the Godfather of it all. Not that we are saying that he had anything to do with the Mafia, OK?

Eleven Jokes about Dead Musicians

Jerry Garcia wakes up in a white room surrounded by musical instruments. He sees Jimi Hendrix and Eric Clapton pick up guitars, then John Lennon sits down at a piano and Janis Joplin, Buddy Holly and Elvis line up at microphones. 'Wow!' says Jerry. 'There really is a rock 'n' roll Heaven, and I'm going to jam with the band!' Hearing this, Elvis leans over and says, 'Heaven?' Just then, Karen Carpenter enters the room and sits down at the drums. 'OK, everybody,' she says, '"Close to You." One, two . . .'

Police at the scene of Sonny Bono's fatal accident reported that it was a quick death. Just like his solo career.

Q: Why did Paula Yates like Michael Hutchence?
A: Because he was well hung.

Right after John Lennon died and went to heaven, Jesus came to him and said, 'So, that crack about being more popular than me . . .'

The remaining members of Pink Floyd get in a car wreck and all three die. They are standing in front of the Pearly Gates when Saint Peter comes up and says, 'Oh, hi, guys! We've been expecting you. You're really going to love it here; this is a great place – and did you know that we even have our own band? We have Elvis Presley singing, Hendrix is playing guitar, Sinatra is on piano and Roger Waters, your old bandmate, is writing lyrics for us!' David Gilmour replies, 'Roger is here? When did he die?' Saint Peter leans over and whispers in his ear: 'It's really God, but he thinks he's Roger Waters!'

Q: If you threw a drummer and a lead singer off a cliff, which would hit the ground first?
A: The singer – the drummer would have to stop halfway down to ask directions.

Saint Peter is greeting people at the gates to heaven. 'What did you do on earth?' he asks one man.
   'I was a doctor,' says the man.
   Saint Peter says, 'Great, go right through the Pearly Gates and on down the golden streets. Next! What did you do on earth?'
   'I was a school teacher,' says the next person.
   'Wonderful,' says Saint Peter, 'Go right on through the Pearly Gates. Next! And what did you do on earth?'
   'I was a soundman,' says the man.
   Saint Peter says, 'Go around the side, up the freight elevator and through the kitchen.'

P. Diddy, Britney Spears and Eminem all die and go to hell. The Devil takes Britney in his hands and she melts into a puddle. Then he takes P. Diddy in his hands and he melts into a puddle. Then he takes Eminem in his hands, but he doesn't melt. The Devil says, 'Why didn't you melt like the other two?' He says, 'Because Eminem melts in your mouth, not in your hands.'

A soundman dies and is met by an angel at the gates to heaven. 'I've got good news and bad news,' the angel says. 'The good news is you get to do sound on the best equipment for the rest of eternity. You will never have to re-eq the room and no one will ever ask for more in the monitors. The bad news is that Saint Peter has a girlfriend and he thinks she can sing.'

Q: What were Kurt Cobain's last words?
A: 'Hole is really going to be big.'

Q: What did Courtney Love say when she came home?
A: 'Who ordered the pizza?'

DISCELLANY

Eleven Rock Stars who *Might* Have Seen a UFO

Reg Presley (The Troggs)
Reg claims to have seen eleven UFOs, plus two other 'elliptical craft'. It's not clear to us why he doesn't just call it thirteen UFOs – but boy, are we glad.

Ray Dorset (Mungo Jerry)
Ray saw ten (only ten!) small creatures 'around four feet tall' crossing the road in front of his car. Our sources do not reveal whether these creatures were led by an eleventh, taller creature, carrying a mysterious 'disc on a pole'.

Noddy Holder (Slade)
Noddy saw a gigantic flying saucer in Bournemouth. Possibly filled with retired aliens.

Lemmy
The Motörhead bass-mangler saw a UFO during his touring days with Hawkwind. He assures us that it couldn't have been an acid-fuelled hallucination because the whole band saw it. It just isn't possible that *all* of Hawkwind were on drugs.

David Byrne
David passes out questionnaires at parties enquiring after other people's UFO experiences. He was also once abducted by his own suit.

Sting
The tantric teacher once saw the top of a mountain 'lit up like a Christmas tree', and ascribed the experience to a UFO visitation. Maybe his chakras were just a little bit out of tune.

John Lennon
During John's notorious 'black-out year' he saw a very unusual aircraft in New York. There's a reference to it on his *Walls & Bridges* album cover. There's no reference to how much John was drinking at the time.

Michael Jackson
The plastic prince has reputedly built a UFO landing strip on a ranch he owns in Nevada. Now there's a man who's starting to believe his own press.

Marc Bolan
During his hippie period, Marc saw 'quite a few' saucers at Glastonbury. We're pretty sure we would have, too, if we'd just inhaled the air in Marc's tent.

Kirk Brandon (Spear of Destiny)
'I've seen a UFO once, with my mother, who's the most down-to-earth person in the world. Even she admitted there was something there.' With his *mum*. Bless.

Gary Numan
'Von Daniken blew it by falsifying the evidence. His theory that God was an astronaut has a lot going for it. A girlfriend and I saw a UFO once. It was like an upside-down pyramid shape.' We've seen some pretty rum things too, Gary. One of them's on your head.

Britney versus Christina: Eleven Opinions

We trawled the Internet to try once and for all to clear up this crucial issue. We wouldn't want to get on the wrong side of any of these fans – they sure don't mince their words (and they are *totally* illiterate) . . .

'Britney is always showing her body on her MTV scenes, especially her new music video, titled DON'T LET ME BE THE LAST TO KNOW, it's a grooowsss to me. YUCK! For me Chistina RULZZZZZZ!!!'

'i think briney spears is dumb because shes to poshy and look like shes wereing a bekine and g-string christina aguilera rules.'

'if you see christina and hear the dumb things she says you can tell that she is a total brat ! so i say that none of them are great or even good! GO

BLINK 182!!!!! ROCK ON!!!!!! I LUV U CODY!!!! I LOVE U CARSON TRL ROCKZ!!!!!!!'

'Britney shows too much skin!! Cristeena might not have any new albums yet but she will and she scuttaly dosen't show so much skin!! And she has an aewsome vocie!!!'

'I like SPEARS better then big puffey hair Chrstina Aguilera beacaus Brinty doesn't have a big affro at a concert the big sence is her affro and brinty at her concert they will look at her not her hair.'

'Brittney Spears dresses like all she wears is bathing suits! She is not a good role-model for kids . . . Even though Cristina sometimes waers stuff that show's too much skin, Cristina Rules!!! Britney Drools!!! Britney doesn't have a chance!!!'

'i THINK CHRISTINA IS BETTER BECAUSE SHE DOOESNT COPY OFF OF THE ROLLING STONES.The song sadisfackcion was made before brittany spears. And brintey was on pepsi camersal and i don't like pepsi.And chritina 's durector is better because he's the nicetist.'

'Christina has a voice so strong and powerful, Britney can't even come close to compare. and also, have you seen Britney's video for her latest song? What's with the lying on some beach, making out with a male supermodle? I think the video is pointless, and inappropriate for kids! So therefor, I think Christina is the best! And,NO,I do not like girls lying on the beach, making out with supermodles. . .like Britney!'

'britney spears lip sings and christina aguilera doesnt. so if u go to britneys concerts your just getttin ripped off! cause she's not really singin. but they both are really cool and popular. theres just stuff that britney needs to change like the breast inplants the lip singing and stuff like that. christina doesnt have all that. they are both cool but if i had to pick which i liked more it would be christina!!!'

'Britney is a great dancer and a role model for me because she takes time out of her schedule to go see her sisters recitle that's why she only had 2 days to make the music video for lucky. As for what i think Britney rules and nobody could change my mind!!!!!!!:-'

And finally there came from the wwwilderness a voice with which we could all agree . . .

'They both stink a lot.'

Eleven Rock Ailments . . .

Addiction to love
A nasty one, this, known to some by its Latin name of *Robertus Palmeritis*. The most obvious symptom of being addicted to love is that your backing band suddenly all start looking the same, more specifically female with slicked-back hair, black dresses and a touch too much make-up. Other symptoms include your mind no longer being your own and the inability to 'ber-reathe'. This is a bit like being unable to breathe, except slightly more elongated, in order to make a line scan.

Fever
An illness that afflicts female singers, particularly those who have been successful in one decade (say the eighties) and less so in the next. What happens is that the singer, shorn of decent new musical ideas and reduced to coming up with stuff like 'Hanky Panky', decides to cover an old Peggy Lee track in a desperate attempt to cure themselves by association with what is technically known as a 'tune'. This is, obviously, a short-term remedy; the recommended long-term solution is a course of young dance producers.

Cold sweat
A condition which James Brown has suffered for many years now. Early indications of the illness are punctuated by groans and grunts. More severe cases include talking to someone called 'Bobby', and by the time you're requesting that people 'hit me now', you know you're in trouble. The cold sweat itself appears to break out when James is kissed. The simple answer is don't kiss him.

Love sickness
An illness that befalls the elder statesmen of rock, most noticeably Bob Dylan on his 1997 album *Time Out of Mind*. It's really an accumulation of more than thirty years of romantic times, a delayed reaction to the heady, simple days of 'I Want You' and 'Lay Lady Lay' being tangled up in blue. To the uninitiated, the effect can be that of the voice sounding increasingly nasal. But really the condition is more simple: an increasingly erratic quality of songwriting.

Being killed by too much love
Not so much an illness, this time, as a warning about over-consumption. Love, like staying out in the sun, is all very well for a while, but overindulge and death by romance is yours. To our knowledge, no one has yet died from overexposure to love, though those with poodle perms are particularly at risk (as spotted on one Brian May).

Crying oneself blind

As documented by Primal Scream on *Give Out But Don't Give Up*, crying oneself blind is a particular danger for those who suffer from the blues. What happens, we believe, is that, to borrow Band Aid's description, the 'bitter sting' of the tears causes the eyes to stop functioning. This is quite different to the bitter tears of Sting, shed when the former Police front-man was upset at 'Walking on the Moon' only reaching number two.

A bad case of loving you

If Robert Palmer isn't addicted to love per se, he certainly needs a remedy for his bad case of loving you. The symptoms are not pleasant: some doctors describe the effects as 'lumpen', others as 'hoary'. One simple cure would be to 'tighten up': forget letting your hair down; instead, re-knot the tie and smooth it down with something like 'She Makes My Day'. Alternatively, come up with a different lyrical idea to the consistent use of medical metaphors.

Social disease

A dangerous condition that, as the name suggests, can affect whole swathes of society. Sufferers start by finding themselves slippery when wet and, before they know it, their hair is starting to both bleach and perm, their jeans have begun to rip at the knees and they're hallucinating about being cowboys. Beware: some supposed cures turn out to be merely bad medicine, serving only to increase the pumping of the air, the cry of 'awwwwwright' and general other forms of jovi-al behaviour.

The bends

This is what happens to a fledgling rock band when they achieve success too quickly. The symptom of the rapid initial rise is ironically known as 'Creep', and has the effect of pigeonholing the group and potentially leaving them forever cursed as the 'Creep band'. The band must then go away and write a fantastic second album. This deals with 'Creep' in the short term but creates a dangerous long-term side effect: the urge to come up with difficult future albums and the subsequent inevitable shedding of fans.

Achy breaky heart

A heart condition that is known to afflict country 'n' western singers, particularly those with lumberjack shirts and mullet haircuts. What happens is that the singer starts filling their songs with words like 'achy' and 'breaky'. This habit acts as an irritant for anyone who hears the song and is potentially life-threatening for the singer, because everyone wants to kill him.

Being out of your mind
A tragic mental condition to which former members of girl bands are particularly susceptible. First, the singer becomes delusional about having a solo career; this quickly escalates into her being taken over by a strong craving for credibility. Although the condition mainly affects the brain, there is also an unfortunate effect on the sufferer's toilet behaviour. Every time the singer wants a number one, she has a number two instead.

And Eleven Rock Doctors to Cure Them

Dr and the Medics
Some doctors are extra cautious about giving bad news, but not this one. Before you know it, he's giving you the low-down about spirits in the sky and what will happen when you've been laid to rest. And you only went to see him because you had hay fever.

Dr John
This doctor taps out his prescriptions on his keyboard.

Dr Feelgood
Although his name suggests a great record of curing patients, in fact his recommendation of combining milk and alcohol is best avoided.

Dr Robert
The 1960s model knew better than to recommend the use of leeches. Only just, mind; his preferred treatment is a course of Beatles to help you through. If it's looking really bad, he might just suggest a revolver.

Dr Robert
The 1980s version was a little less conventional, and was struck off for his controversial treatments involving blowing and monkeys.

Rock and Roll Doctor
A specialist chiropodist, specifically aimed at those people who have Little Feat.

Docteur Jeykll et Monsieur Hyde
A French practitioner used by Serge Gainsbourg, who was similarly possessed of a double personality. One part of him was obsessed with love making, while the other's passion was for making love.

Dr Mabuse
A German consultant used by, among others, Frankie stablemates Propaganda. Best known for his work on that curious eighties stomach complaint the Zang Tum Tum.

Dr Beat
He is Florida's finest, and he puts all his faith in a device known as the Miami Sound Machine. Although it worked for a number of years to reasonable success, some patients suffered the side effect of being unable to help moving their feet.

Doctor Doctor
The medical antidote to seeing double, technically known as Thompson Twinning. Great for when you are hurting hurting or having strange dreams about being a detective.

Dr Hook
A first-class doctor of love, Hooky is full of advice for those in love with a beautiful woman. Has a sideline as an optician, making specialist contact lenses that give the wearer sexy eyes.

Eleven Rock Roads

'Alphabet St' by Prince
But is it in the *A-Z*?

'Electric Avenue' by Eddie Grant
For cars with the right reggae-stration number.

'The Road to Hell' by Chris Rea
The M25. With Auberge on the radio.

'303' by Kula Shaker
The A303, which goes to Somerset. Kula Shaker just went.

'Thunder Road' by Bruce Springsteen
Great if your car goes like greased lightning.

'Route 66' by The Rolling Stones
Where you get your kicks.

'M62 Song' by The Doves
Horrible road. Great song.

'Positively 4th Street' by Bob Dylan
If you're riding a motorbike, be careful.

'Highway to Hell' by AC/DC
The Australian version of the Road to Hell. Auberge is probably still on the radio.

'Autobahn' by Kraftwerk
You don't have to keep to the speed limit.

'Road to Nowhere' by Talking Heads
Please insert gratuitous joke about rock star in car crash at this point.

Eleven Band Names Containing Unnecessary Punk2-a'tion

Wham!
Exclaimed the eighties pop crown princes.

D:ream
Colonic irritation.

Therapy?
There was, for us, a question mark over their music.

Hear'say
No reason for it. A little like the band.

B*witched
Small star in the name. Small stars they stayed.

5ive
Thought they were 1derful. Utterly 4gettable.

Menswe@r
Not exactly where it's @.

Hurricane #1
We had their number.

Was (Not Was)
Bracketed with late-eighties pop.

*NSync
*NDescribably bad.

!!!
We don't know how we're meant to pronounce this. We don't really care.

Eleven Country 'n' Western Songs to Cover All Bases

Whatever stage of your life you are at, you can bet your bottom yankee dollar that the ten-gallon hat brigade have a song for it. We won't bother you with the artists' names because you wouldn't believe us anyway . . .

On love at first sight
'Her Teeth Were Stained, but Her Heart Was Pure'

On the gentle art of wooing
'She's Actin' Single and I'm Drinkin' Doubles'

On that first date
'I Wouldn't Take Her to a Dog Fight, 'Cause I'm Afraid She'd Win'

On kissing
'We Used to Kiss on the Lips, But It's All Over Now'

On that first night of passion
'I Got in at 2 with a 10 and Woke Up at 10 with a 2'

On murder
'If I Had Shot You When I Wanted to, I'd Be Out by Now'

On religion
'I've Been Drop-Kicked by Jesus Through the Goalposts of Life'

On having children
'You're the Reason Our Kids Are so Ugly'

On violence
'I Gave Her My Heart and a Diamond and She Clubbed Me With a Spade'

On infidelity
'I Just Bought a Car from a Guy That Stole My Girl, But the Car Don't Run So I Figure We're Even'

On breaking up
'When You Wrapped My Lunch in a Road Map, I Knew You Meant Good-Bye'

Eleven Reasons Why Elvis Might Be Jesus

(Just think how much more fun that annual trip to church would be!)

Jesus said, 'Love thy neighbour' (Matthew 22:39), and Elvis said, 'Don't be cruel'.

Jesus is part of the 'Trinity' and Elvis's first band was a trio.

Jesus walked on water (Matthew 14:25) and Elvis surfed (*Blue Hawaii*, Paramount, 1965).

Jesus's entourage, the Apostles, had twelve members, as did Elvis's entourage, the Memphis Mafia.

Jesus was resurrected and Elvis had the famous *1968 Comeback Special*.

Jesus said, 'If any man thirst, let him come unto me, and drink' (John 7:37), and Elvis said, 'Drinks on me!' (*Jailhouse Rock*, MGM, 1957).

Matthew was one of Jesus's biographers ('The Gospel of Matthew') and Neil Matthews was one of Elvis's biographers (*Elvis: A Golden Tribute*).

'Jesus's clothes became a dazzling white' (Mark 9:3), and Elvis's snow-white jumpsuits dazzled his audiences.

Jesus lived in a state of grace in a Near-Eastern land, while Elvis lived in Graceland in a nearly eastern state.

Jesus was the Lamb of God, whereas Elvis had mutton-chop sideburns.

Jesus said, 'Man shall not live by bread alone,' and Elvis liked peanut butter and banana sandwiches.

Eleven Things to Celebrate during the Eurovision Song Contest

Love it or loathe it, there is only one way to park your Euro-scepticism and get through this annual celebration of chest-hair, glitter paint and bad-hair muzak. By getting drunk.

Raise your glass every time you see any of the following:

The female presenter's dress changes.

The presenters overlapping with the voters during the video/audio link because of the bad delay.

A grossly overweight lead singer.

Germany sparing *one single point* for her southern neighbour, Austria.

A singer from Eastern Europe with fake blonde hair.

Visible/prominent nipples/genitalia.

An act with ideas stolen from Eurovision acts of previous years.

Dancing that surpasses belief and credibility.

A singer flirting with the camera when she has finished her song.

Acts speaking on their mobile phones to their families during voting.

Reference made to Norway's *nul points*.

By now Ireland will have won again and you should be beyond caring. Goodnight.

Eleven Rock Questions

One sometimes wonders why rock 'n' roll lyrics are better at asking questions than answering them. Like Hazel Dean, we are still searching for the answers to these intellectual quandaries . . .

Who the f*** is Alice?

Why do fools fall in love?

Why does it always rain on me?

Who let the dogs out?

What's the frequency, Kenneth?

What becomes of the broken-hearted?

What difference does it make?

What have I done to deserve this?

What time is love?

When will I be famous?

Who's zooming who?

If you know the answers to any of the above, do email juanlauda@rockandpopelevens.com.

Eleven Reasons Why We Love Spiñal Tap

This is Spiñal Tap is the comedic brainchild of director Rob Reiner and writers Christopher Guest, Michael McKean and Harry Shearer. (These four created Spiñal Tap for a 1979 ABC-TV sketch-comedy effort called *The TV Show*.) Pure and simple, this rockumentary is absolute genius in its merciless lampooning of the ever-prevalent notion of faded rock stars touring on and on until they split up and then re-form for the inevitable pension-top-up reunion tour. Men as old as your dad, wearing leather trousers, trying to be cool, rocking out and eyeing the chicks. *This is Spinal Tap* contains more home truths about life on tour than anything else out there, is laugh-out-loud funny and a must-have for any tour-bus video collection. To pick just eleven best bits is to do the film a disservice, but pick eleven we must. Kings of rock 'n' roll, let us now salute you . . .

We love the 'Hello, Cleveland' sequence
Where the band gets lost in the labyrinthine corridors of the Xanadu Star Theater, Cleveland, and can't find the stage. Priceless.

We love the 'Who's in here – no one?' scene
In which the bread on the food platter in the band room is too small to fold and only some of the olives have pimento filling.

We love the scene when they turn up to play a festival
When they arrive they discover that they have been given second billing to the puppet show. The reassurance that they have been given the bigger dressing room doesn't appear to help matters much.

We love the scene with the Stonehenge model
Anjelica Huston's character has designed a scale model of Stonehenge which is lowered on to the stage during the song 'Stonehenge', only for the band to discover that their manager inadvertently asked for it to be 18 inches rather than 18 feet tall. The arrival of some pipe-playing dwarves compounds matters. On a recent real-life live tour, the tiny little Stonehenge model refused to go back up into the rafters from whence it came. Strangely enough, it was a *real* problem, not one set up in advance by the band.

We love the pod malfunction
Where bass player Derek Smalls gets trapped in a large Perspex pod in full view of the audience.

We love David St Hubbins' nightmare girlfriend, Jeanine
She turns up and redesigns the band's costumes according to their signs of the zodiac.

We love the herpes
It spreads through the band like wildfire after an encounter with a particularly virulent groupie.

We love Derek Smalls in the airport security scan
He continuously sets off the scanning machine until he reveals an aluminium-foil-covered cucumber down his trousers.

We love inept Artie Fufkin
The Midwest PR guy for Polymer Records who is responsible for a disastrous signing session for the *Smell the Glove* album to which no one turns up.

We love 'Sex Farm' topping the Japanese charts
After their career has collapsed in the US, they are suddenly reunited with fame and each other when their version of 'Sex Farm' tops the Japanese hit parade.

And above all we love the Marshall amp that goes up to eleven
Nigel Tufnel shows Marty DiBergi around his guitar collection and reveals the Holy Grail.

Biographies and Acknowledgements

Simon Trewin was eleven in 1977 when The Sex Pistols' 'God Save the Queen' was kept off the top spot by Rod Stewart. He works as a literary agent in London representing some of the people who appear in this book and wants to make it clear that all the bad things said about them were written by his co-authors. He would like to thank his lovely wife Helen (for going up to twelve – so far), his cool son Jack (for being eleven), Claire Gill (for coping), the legendary Purple Gangster Geoff Bowyer (for making him laugh), co-authors Michael and Tom (good men to have on your side), and Leo (top cat). Simon still has 30GB free on his iPod.

Michael Moran was eleven in 1971, the year that Benny Hill had the Christmas number one with 'Ernie'. In his picaresque journey through life he has been employed variously as a recording artiste, lingerie salesman, record producer, journalist and knitwear model. He has a column in *Word* magazine which contains regular updates on the state of his iPod. He would like to thank his lovely wife, Cassie (without whom it would have been impossible), and his adorable daughter, Leah (without whom it would be pointless). He feels indebted to everyone who has contributed to his career to date, not least his two co-authors. May all your amps go to infinity.

Tom Bromley was eleven in 1983, the year in which, as so rightly pointed out by Kajagoogoo, it was ooh to be ah. The author of two novels, a very nice new book about one-hit wonders and various ghostwritten tomes, he has a remote control for his iPod which Michael gave him – and very flash it is too. He would like to thank his wife, Joanna, who gets eleven out of ten for putting up with him. Oh, and Simon and Michael. Just because.

The authors would also like to thank: Juan Lauda at the *Rock and Pop Elevens* HQ, Special Agent Jim Gill at PFD, Monica O'Connell, and Lindsay, Kate, Gina and the team at Michael O'Mara for making it one louder.

This is the first of eleven volumes and your comments are very welcome:
www.rockandpopelevens.com

COMING SOON:

Celebrity Elevens